PENGUIN BOOKS

THE SOLACE OF OPEN SPACES

Gretel Ehrlich was born and raised in California and first went to Wyoming as a documentary filmmaker. She began to write full time in 1979 and has also worked on ranches lambing, branding, herding sheep, and calving.

She was educated at Bennington College, UCLA Film School, and the New School for Social Research. Her prose pieces have appeared in *The New York Times*, *The Atlantic*, *Harper's*, and *New Age Journal*. She has also published two books of poetry, and a story collection (with Edward Hoagland), *City Tales, Wyoming Stories*.

Gretel Ehrlich has received awards from the National Endowment for the Arts and the Wyoming Council for the Arts. She lives with her husband on a ranch in Shell, Wyoming.

THE SOLACE OF OPEN SPACES

GRETEL EHRLICH

PENGUIN BOOKS

PENGUIN BOOKS
Published by the Penguin Group
Viking Penguin Inc., 40 West 23rd Street, New York, New York 10010, U.S.A.
Penguin Books Ltd, 27 Wrights Lane, London W8 5TZ, England
Penguin Books Australia Ltd, Ringwood, Victoria, Australia
Penguin Books Canada Ltd, 2801 John Street,
Markham, Ontario, Canada L3R 1B4
Penguin Books (N.Z.) Ltd, 182–190 Wairau Road,
Auckland 10, New Zealand

Penguin Books Ltd, Registered Offices:
Harmondsworth, Middlesex, England

First published in the United States of America by Viking Penguin Inc. 1985
Published in Penguin Books 1986

7   9   10   8

The author wishes to thank the National Endowment for the Arts for their assistance.

Special thanks goes to Suzanne Mantell
for early and continued encouragement and editorial advice.

Portions of this book appeared originally, in slightly different form, in *The Atlantic*,
The New York Times, *New Age Journal*, and the *Caspar Star Journal*.

Grateful acknowledgment is made to Farrar, Straus and Giroux, Inc., for permission
to reprint four lines from "Strophes," from *A Part of Speech*, by Joseph Brodsky.
Copyright © 1973, 1974, 1975, 1976, 1977, 1978, 1979, 1980 by Farrar, Straus and
Giroux, Inc.

LIBRARY OF CONGRESS CATALOGING IN PUBLICATION DATA
Ehrlich, Gretel.
The solace of open spaces.
Contents: The solace of open spaces—Obituary—
Other lives—[etc.]
1. Ehrlich, Gretel—Homes and haunts—Wyoming.
2. Authors, American—20th century—Biography.
3. Wyoming—Description and travel.   I. Title.
[PS3555.H72Z476   1986]   814'.54   86-9514
ISBN 0 14 00.8113 5

Drawing by Isabelle A. Carlhian

Printed in the United States of America
Set in Granjon

For my parents,
and
for Press,
with love

Life's a freewheeling vendor:
occiput, penis, knee.
And geography blended
with time equals destiny.

—JOSEPH BRODSKY

PREFACE

This book was begun in 1979 and finished in 1984. Originally conceived as a straight-through narrative, it was instead written in fits and starts and later arranged chronologically.

It is impossible to speak of writing this book without mentioning the circumstances and transitions taking place in my life at the time. Beginning in 1976, when I went to Wyoming to make a film, I had the experience of waking up not knowing where I was, whether I was a man or a woman, or which toothbrush was mine. I had suffered a tragedy and made a drastic geographical and cultural move fairly baggageless, but I wasn't losing my grip. As Jim Bridger is reported to have said, "I wasn't lost, I just didn't know where I was for a few weeks." What I *had* lost (at least for a while) was my appetite for the life I had left: city surroundings, old friends, familiar comforts. It had occurred to me that comfort was only a disguise for discomfort; reference points, a disguise for what will always change.

Friends asked when I was going to stop "hiding out" in Wyoming. What appeared to them as a landscape of lunar desolation and intellectual backwardness was luxurious to me. For the first time I was able to take up residence on earth with no alibis, no self-promoting schemes.

The beginnings of this book took the form of raw journal entries sent to a friend in Hawaii. I chose her because she had been raised in a trailerhouse behind a bar in Wyoming; she then made the outlandish leap to a tropical climate and a life in academia. I was jumping in the opposite direction and suspected we might have crossed paths midair somewhere.

The sudden changes in my life brought on the usual zany dreams: road blocks were set up where I walked barefoot with a big suitcase; national boundaries changed overnight and I was forced to take a long, arbitrary detour. The detour, of course, became the actual path; the digressions in my writing, the narrative.

The truest art I would strive for in any work would be to give the page the same qualities as earth: weather would land on it harshly; light would elucidate the most difficult truths; wind would sweep away obtuse padding. Finally, the lessons of impermanence taught me this: loss constitutes an odd kind of fullness; despair empties out into an unquenchable appetite for life.

The narrative that follows has an overlapping chronology. It is riprap and does, I hope, form a hard roadbed. But as with all major detours, all lessons of impermanence, what might have been a straight shot is full of bumps and bends.

CONTENTS

THE SOLACE OF
OPEN SPACES

It's May and I've just awakened from a nap, curled against sagebrush the way my dog taught me to sleep—sheltered from wind. A front is pulling the huge sky over me, and from the dark a hailstone has hit me on the head. I'm trailing a band of two thousand sheep across a stretch of Wyoming badlands, a fifty-mile trip that takes five days because sheep shade up in hot sun and won't budge until it's cool. Bunched together now, and excited into a run by the storm, they drift across dry land, tumbling into draws like water and surge out again onto the rugged, choppy plateaus that are the building blocks of this state.

The name Wyoming comes from an Indian word meaning "at the great plains," but the plains are really valleys, great arid valleys, sixteen hundred square miles, with the horizon bending up on all sides into mountain ranges. This gives the vastness a sheltering look.

Winter lasts six months here. Prevailing winds spill snow-drifts to the east, and new storms from the northwest re-plenish them. This white bulk is sometimes dizzying, even nauseating, to look at. At twenty, thirty, and forty degrees below zero, not only does your car not work, but neither do your mind and body. The landscape hardens into a dungeon of space. During the winter, while I was riding to find a new calf, my jeans froze to the saddle, and in the silence that such cold creates I felt like the first person on earth, or the last.

Today the sun is out—only a few clouds billowing. In the east, where the sheep have started off without me, the benchland tilts up in a series of eroded red-earthed mesas, planed flat on top by a million years of water; behind them, a bold line of muscular scarps rears up ten thousand feet to become the Big Horn Mountains. A tidal pattern is engraved into the ground, as if left by the sea that once covered this state. Canyons curve down like galaxies to meet the oncoming rush of flat land.

To live and work in this kind of open country, with its hundred-mile views, is to lose the distinction between background and foreground. When I asked an older ranch hand to describe Wyoming's openness, he said, "It's all a bunch of nothing—wind and rattlesnakes—and so much of it you can't tell where you're going or where you've been and it don't make much difference." John, a sheepman I know, is tall and handsome and has an explosive temperament. He has a perfect intuition about people and sheep. They call him "Highpockets," because he's so long-legged; his graceful stride matches the distances he has to cover. He says, "Open space hasn't affected me at all. It's all the people moving in on it." The huge ranch he was born on takes up much of one county and spreads into another state; to put 100,000 miles on his pickup in three years and never leave home is not unusual. A friend of mine has an aunt who ranched on Powder River and didn't go off her place for eleven years. When her husband died, she quickly moved to town, bought a car, and drove around the States to see what she'd been missing.

Most people tell me they've simply driven through Wyoming, as if there were nothing to stop for. Or else they've skied in Jackson Hole, a place Wyomingites acknowledge uncomfortably because its green beauty and chic affluence are mismatched with the rest of the state. Most of Wyoming has a "lean-to" look. Instead of big, roomy barns and Victorian houses, there are dugouts, low sheds, log cabins, sheep camps, and fence lines that look like driftwood blown haphazardly into place. People here still feel pride because they live in such a harsh place, part of the glamorous cowboy past, and they are determined not to be the victims of a mining-dominated future.

Most characteristic of the state's landscape is what a developer euphemistically describes as "indigenous growth right up to your front door"—a reference to waterless stands of salt sage, snakes, jack rabbits, deerflies, red dust, a brief respite of wildflowers, dry washes, and no trees. In the Great Plains the vistas look like music, like Kyries of grass, but Wyoming seems to be the doing of a mad architect—tumbled and twisted, ribboned with faded, deathbed colors, thrust up and pulled down as if the place had been startled out of a deep sleep and thrown into a pure light.

I came here four years ago. I had not planned to stay, but I couldn't make myself leave. John, the sheepman, put me to work immediately. It was spring, and shearing time. For fourteen days of fourteen hours each, we moved thousands of sheep through sorting corrals to be sheared, branded, and deloused. I suspect that my original motive for coming here was to "lose myself" in new and unpopulated territory. Instead of producing the numbness I thought I wanted, life on the sheep ranch woke me up. The vitality of the people I was working with flushed out what had become a hallucinatory rawness inside me. I threw away my clothes and bought new ones; I cut my hair. The arid country was a clean slate. Its absolute indifference steadied me.

Sagebrush covers 58,000 square miles of Wyoming. The biggest city has a population of fifty thousand, and there are only five settlements that could be called cities in the whole state. The rest are towns, scattered across the expanse with as much as sixty miles between them, their populations two thousand, fifty, or ten. They are fugitive-looking, perched on a barren, windblown bench, or tagged onto a river or a rail-road, or laid out straight in a farming valley with implement stores and a block-long Mormon church. In the eastern part of the state, which slides down into the Great Plains, the new mining settlements are boomtowns, trailer cities, metal knots on flat land.

Despite the desolate look, there's a coziness to living in this state. There are so few people (only 470,000) that ranchers who buy and sell cattle know one another statewide; the kids who choose to go to college usually go to the state's one university, in Laramie; hired hands work their way around Wyoming in a lifetime of hirings and firings. And despite the physical separation, people stay in touch, often driving two or three hours to another ranch for dinner.

Seventy-five years ago, when travel was by buckboard or horseback, cowboys who were temporarily out of work rode the grub line—drifting from ranch to ranch, mending fences or milking cows, and receiving in exchange a bed and meals. Gossip and messages traveled this slow circuit with them, creating an intimacy between ranchers who were three and four weeks' ride apart. One old-time couple I know, whose turn-of-the-century homestead was used by an outlaw gang as a relay station for stolen horses, recall that if you were traveling, desperado or not, any lighted ranch house was a welcome sign. Even now, for someone who lives in a remote spot, arriving at a ranch or coming to town for supplies is cause for celebration. To emerge from isolation can be disorienting. Everything looks bright, new, vivid. After I had been herding sheep for only three days, the sound of the camp tender's pickup flustered me. Longing for human company, I felt a foolish grin take over my face; yet I had to resist an urgent temptation to run and hide.

Things happen suddenly in Wyoming, the change of seasons and weather; for people, the violent swings in and out of isolation. But good-naturedness is concomitant with severity. Friendliness is a tradition. Strangers passing on the road wave hello. A common sight is two pickups stopped side by side far out on a range, on a dirt track winding through the sage. The drivers will share a cigarette, uncap their thermos bottles, and pass a battered cup, steaming with coffee, between windows. These meetings summon up the details of several generations, because, in Wyoming, private histories are largely public knowledge.

Because ranch work is a physical and, these days, economic strain, being "at home on the range" is a matter of vigor, self-reliance, and common sense. A person's life is not a series of dramatic events for which he or she is applauded or exiled but a slow accumulation of days, seasons, years, fleshed out by the generational weight of one's family and anchored by a land-bound sense of place.

In most parts of Wyoming, the human population is visibly outnumbered by the animal. Not far from my town of fifty, I rode into a narrow valley and startled a herd of two hundred elk. Eagles look like small people as they eat car-killed deer by the road. Antelope, moving in small, graceful bands, travel at sixty miles an hour, their mouths open as if drinking in the space.

The solitude in which westerners live makes them quiet. They telegraph thoughts and feelings by the way they tilt their heads and listen; pulling their Stetsons into a steep dive over their eyes, or pigeon-toeing one boot over the other, they lean against a fence with a fat wedge of Copenhagen beneath their lower lips and take in the whole scene. These detached looks of quiet amusement are sometimes cynical, but they can also come from a dry-eyed humility as lucid as the air is clear.

Conversation goes on in what sounds like a private code; a few phrases imply a complex of meanings. Asking directions, you get a curious list of details. While trailing sheep I was told to "ride up to that kinda upturned rock, follow the pink wash, turn left at the dump, and then you'll see the water hole." One friend told his wife on roundup to "turn at the salt lick and the dead cow," which turned out to be a scattering of bones and no salt lick at all.

Sentence structure is shortened to the skin and bones of a thought. Descriptive words are dropped, even verbs; a cowboy looking over a corral full of horses will say to a wrangler, "Which one needs rode?" People hold back their thoughts in what seems to be a dumbfounded silence, then erupt with an excoriating perceptive remark. Language, so compressed, becomes metaphorical. A rancher ended a relationship with one remark: "You're a bad check," meaning bouncing in and out was intolerable, and even coming back would be no good.

What's behind this laconic style is shyness. There is no vocabulary for the subject of feelings. It's not a hangdog shyness, or anything coy—always there's a robust spirit in evidence behind the restraint, as if the earth-dredging wind that pulls across Wyoming had carried its people's voices away but everything else in them had shouldered confidently into the breeze.

I've spent hours riding to sheep camp at dawn in a pickup when nothing was said; eaten meals in the cookhouse when the only words spoken were a mumbled "Thank you, ma'am" at the end of dinner. The silence is profound. Instead of talking, we seem to share one eye. Keenly observed, the world is transformed. The landscape is engorged with detail, every movement on it chillingly sharp. The air between people is charged. Days unfold, bathed in their own music. Nights become hallucinatory; dreams, prescient.

Spring weather is capricious and mean. It snows, then blisters with heat. There have been tornadoes. They lay their elephant trunks out in the sage until they find houses, then slurp everything up and leave. I've noticed that melting snowbanks hiss and rot, viperous, then drip into calm pools where ducklings hatch and livestock, being trailed to summer range, drink. With the ice cover gone, rivers churn a milkshake brown, taking culverts and small bridges with them. Water in such an arid place (the average annual rainfall where I live is less than eight inches) is like blood. It festoons drab land with green veins; a line of cottonwoods following a stream; a strip of alfalfa; and, on ditch banks, wild asparagus growing.

I've moved to a small cattle ranch owned by friends. It's at the foot of the Big Horn Mountains. A few weeks ago, I helped them deliver a calf who was stuck halfway out of his mother's body. By the time he was freed, we could see a heartbeat, but he was straining against a swollen tongue for air. Mary and I held him upside down by his back feet, while Stan, on his hands and knees in the blood, gave the calf mouth-to-mouth resuscitation. I have a vague memory of being pneumonia-choked as a child, my mother giving me her air, which may account for my romance with this windswept state.

If anything is endemic to Wyoming, it is wind. This big room of space is swept out daily, leaving a bone yard of fossils, agates, and carcasses in every stage of decay. Though it was water that initially shaped the state, wind is the meticulous gardener, raising dust and pruning the sage.

I try to imagine a world in which I could ride my horse across uncharted land. There is no wilderness left; wildness, yes, but true wilderness has been gone on this continent since the time of Lewis and Clark's overland journey.

Two hundred years ago, the Crow, Shoshone, Arapaho, Cheyenne, and Sioux roamed the intermountain West, orchestrating their movements according to hunger, season, and warfare. Once they acquired horses, they traversed the spines of all the big Wyoming ranges—the Absarokas, the Wind Rivers, the Tetons, the Big Horns—and wintered on the unprotected plains that fan out from them. Space was life. The world was their home.

What was life-giving to Native Americans was often

nightmarish to sodbusters who had arrived encumbered with families and ethnic pasts to be transplanted in nearly uninhabitable land. The great distances, the shortage of water and trees, and the loneliness created unexpected hardships for them. In her book *O Pioneers!,* Willa Cather gives a settler's version of the bleak landscape:

The little town behind them had vanished as if it had never been, had fallen behind the swell of the prairie, and the stern frozen country received them into its bosom. The homesteads were few and far apart; here and there a windmill gaunt against the sky, a sod house crouching in a hollow.

The emptiness of the West was for others a geography of possibility. Men and women who amassed great chunks of land and struggled to preserve unfenced empires were, despite their self-serving motives, unwitting geographers. They understood the lay of the land. But by the 1850s the Oregon and Mormon trails sported bumper-to-bumper traffic. Wealthy landowners, many of them aristocratic absentee landlords, known as remittance men because they were paid to come West and get out of their families' hair, overstocked the range with more than a million head of cattle. By 1885 the feed and water were desperately short, and the winter of 1886 laid out the gaunt bodies of dead animals so closely together that when the thaw came, one rancher from Kaycee claimed to have walked on cowhide all the way to Crazy Woman Creek, twenty miles away.

Territorial Wyoming was a boy's world. The land was generous with everything but water. At first there was room enough, food enough, for everyone. And, as with all be-

9

ginnings, an expansive mood set in. The young cowboys, drifters, shopkeepers, schoolteachers, were heroic, lawless, generous, rowdy, and tenacious. The individualism and optimism generated during those times have endured.

John Tisdale rode north with the trail herds from Texas. He was a college-educated man with enough money to buy a small outfit near the Powder River. While driving home from the town of Buffalo with a buckboard full of Christmas toys for his family and a winter's supply of food, he was shot in the back by an agent of the cattle barons who resented the encroachment of small-time stockmen like him. The wealthy cattlemen tried to control all the public grazing land by restricting membership in the Wyoming Stock Growers Association, as if it were a country club. They ostracized from roundups and brandings cowboys and ranchers who were not members, then denounced them as rustlers. Tisdale's death, the second such cold-blooded murder, kicked off the Johnson County cattle war, which was no simple good-guy-bad-guy shoot-out but a complicated class struggle between landed gentry and less affluent settlers—a shocking reminder that the West was not an egalitarian sanctuary after all.

Fencing ultimately enforced boundaries, but barbed wire abrogated space. It was stretched across the beautiful valleys, into the mountains, over desert badlands, through buffalo grass. The "anything is possible" fever—the lure of any new place—was constricted. The integrity of the land as a geographical body, and the freedom to ride anywhere on it, were lost.

I punched cows with a young man named Martin, who is the great-grandson of John Tisdale. His inheritance is not the open land that Tisdale knew and prematurely lost but a rage against restraint.

Wyoming tips down as you head northeast; the highest ground—the Laramie Plains—is on the Colorado border. Up where I live, the Big Horn River leaks into difficult, arid terrain. In the basin where it's dammed, sandhill cranes gather and, with delicate legwork, slice through the stilled water. I was driving by with a rancher one morning when he commented that cranes are "old-fashioned." When I asked why, he said, "Because they mate for life." Then he looked at me with a twinkle in his eyes, as if to say he really did believe in such things but also understood why we break our own rules.

In all this open space, values crystalize quickly. People are strong on scruples but tenderhearted about quirky behavior. A friend and I found one ranch hand, who's "not quite right in the head," sitting in front of the badly decayed carcass of a cow, shaking his finger and saying, "Now, I don't want you to do this ever again!" When I asked what was wrong with him, I was told, "He's goofier than hell, just like the rest of us." Perhaps because the West is historically new, conventional morality is still felt to be less important than rock-bottom truths. Though there's always a lot of teasing and sparring, people are blunt with one another, sometimes even cruel, believing honesty is stronger medicine than sympathy, which may console but often conceals.

The formality that goes hand in hand with the rowdiness is known as the Western Code. It's a list of practical do's and don'ts, faithfully observed. A friend, Cliff, who runs a trap-line in the winter, cut off half his foot while chopping a hole in the ice. Alone, he dragged himself to his pickup and headed for town, stopping to open the ranch gate as he left, and getting out to close it again, thus losing, in his observance of rules, precious time and blood. Later, he commented, "How would it look, them having to come to the hospital to tell me their cows had gotten out?"

Accustomed to emergencies, my friends doctor each other from the vet's bag with relish. When one old-timer suffered a heart attack in hunting camp, his partner quickly stirred up a brew of red horse liniment and hot water and made the half-conscious victim drink it, then tied him onto a horse and led him twenty miles to town. He regained consciousness and lived.

The roominess of the state has affected political attitudes as well. Ranchers keep up with world politics and the convulsions of the economy but are basically isolationists. Being used to running their own small empires of land and livestock, they're suspicious of big government. It's a "don't fence me in" holdover from a century ago. They still want the elbow room their grandfathers had, so they're strongly conservative, but with a populist twist.

Summer is the season when we get our "cowboy tans"—on the lower parts of our faces and on three fourths of our arms. Excessive heat, in the nineties and higher, sends us outside with the mosquitoes. In winter we're tucked inside our houses, and the white wasteland outside appears to be expanding, but in summer all the greenery abridges space.

Summer is a go-ahead season. Every living thing is off the block and in the race: battalions of bugs in flight and biting; bats swinging around my log cabin as if the bases were loaded and someone had hit a home run. Some of summer's high-speed growth is ominous: larkspur, death camas, and green greasewood can kill sheep—an ironic idea, dying in this desert from eating what is too verdant. With sixteen hours of daylight, farmers and ranchers irrigate feverishly. There are first, second, and third cuttings of hay, some crews averaging only four hours of sleep a night for weeks. And, like the cowboys who in summer ride the night rodeo circuit, nighthawks make daredevil dives at dusk with an eerie whirring sound like a plane going down on the shimmering horizon.

In the town where I live, they've had to board up the dance-hall windows because there have been so many fights. There's so little to do except work that people wind up in a state of idle agitation that becomes fatalistic, as if there were nothing to be done about all this untapped energy. So the dark side to the grandeur of these spaces is the small-mindedness that seals people in. Men become hermits; women go mad. Cabin fever explodes into suicides, or into grudges and lifelong family feuds. Two sisters in my area inherited a ranch but found they couldn't get along. They fenced the place in half. When one's cows got out and mixed with the other's, the women went at each other with shovels. They ended up in the same hospital room but never spoke a word to each other for the rest of their lives.

After the brief lushness of summer, the sun moves south. The range grass is brown. Livestock is trailed back down from the mountains. Water holes begin to frost over at night. Last fall Martin asked me to accompany him on a pack trip. With five horses, we followed a river into the mountains behind the tiny Wyoming town of Meeteetse. Groves of aspen, red and orange, gave off a light that made us look toasted. Our hunting camp was so high that clouds skidded across our foreheads, then slowed to sail out across the warm valleys. Except for a bull moose who wandered into our camp and mistook our black gelding for a rival, we shot at nothing.

One of our evening entertainments was to watch the night sky. My dog, a dingo bred to herd sheep, also came on the trip. He is so used to the silence and empty skies that when an airplane flies over he always looks up and eyes the distant intruder quizzically. The sky, lately, seems to be much more crowded than it used to be. Satellites make their silent passes in the dark with great regularity. We counted eighteen in one hour's viewing. How odd to think that while they circumnavigated the planet, Martin and I had moved only six miles into our local wilderness and had seen no other human for the two weeks we stayed there.

At night, by moonlight, the land is whittled to slivers—a ridge, a river, a strip of grassland stretching to the mountains, then the huge sky. One morning a full moon was setting in the west just as the sun was rising. I felt precariously balanced between the two as I loped across a meadow. For a moment, I could believe that the stars, which were still visible, work like cooper's bands, holding together everything above Wyoming.

Space has a spiritual equivalent and can heal what is divided and burdensome in us. My grandchildren will probably use space shuttles for a honeymoon trip or to recover from heart attacks, but closer to home we might also learn how to carry space inside ourselves in the effortless way we carry our skins. Space represents sanity, not a life purified, dull, or "spaced out" but one that might accommodate intelligently any idea or situation.

From the clayey soil of northern Wyoming is mined bentonite, which is used as a filler in candy, gum, and lipstick. We Americans are great on fillers, as if what we have, what we are, is not enough. We have a cultural tendency toward denial, but, being affluent, we strangle ourselves with what we can buy. We have only to look at the houses we build to see how we build *against* space, the way we drink against pain and loneliness. We fill up space as if it were a pie shell, with things whose opacity further obstructs our ability to see what is already there.

OBITUARY

One of the largest sheep ranches in northern Wyoming went under this week. Eight years ago it was a robust community of a hundred or so hired hands employed in a diversified program of beef cattle, farming, and sheep. The auction was held during the height of the lambing season in one of two capacious sheds used for that purpose. It was empty that day for the first time in eighty-seven years. Cliff, the auctioneer, who had worked for the ranch and ran the lambing shed, began the sale: "Used to be, I'd lamb out two hundred ewes a day in here. . . . Well, I guess we better begin." The sheep sold, then the pens, kennels, water troughs, feed bunks, as well as the buildings that housed them. The owners were there, a husband and wife, she a descendant of the original Mormon homesteader. They had the drawn, brittle look that comes from a lifetime of doing work you don't love, then finding out you're a million dollars in debt to boot. "She's got so many wrinkles she has to screw her hat on to go to church," said a sheepherder, now unemployed, as she walked by. Her husband, who had married into the family, squinted as if he had been slapped in the face.

Outside, above the stock trucks that had come to cart things away, clouds stretched vertically, spanning half the sky, and just before a rain squall hit, the light turned violet. A pair of eagles circled above the tin roof as if from habit—in past years there would have been a man-sized dead-pile to pick at. They cocked their heads, scanned the ground, and flew away.

A big ranch is a miniature society. Its demise has the impact of a bankruptcy in a small town: another hundred people out of work and a big chunk of the town's business is suddenly gone. A ranch offers more than jobs; whole families are taken in, their needs attended to: housing, food, schools, even a graveyard plot for those who died on the job or liked the place so much they wanted to be buried there. Itinerant cowboys and sheepherders are given tools of their trade—a horse, a working dog, a saddle, rifle, binoculars—if they arrived empty-handed, and the farm hands are provided with air-conditioned tractors. Altogether, this extended ranch family includes not just cowboys and sheepherders but irrigators, mechanics, camp tenders, foremen, and cooks. A loyal veteran of the outfit would always be assured of a place to live out his days. When he became too old or infirm to work, he might live in the ranch yard and feed the dogs or clear the kosha grass from the pens in the spring. In exchange he could eat in the cookhouse or batch it with a year's supply of elk meat or mutton.

Ben, who had herded sheep and couldn't work after a bout of tick fever, preferred solitude. They pulled his sheep wagon to a remote piece of deeded land twenty miles from town. Because he had no facilities there—no car, running water, or electricity—a plumber from town agreed to bring a weekly supply of groceries, all charged to the ranch. When we sheared sheep below the bluff where Ben lived, we could see him pacing back and forth in front of his wagon like a caged lion, but when I drove up to ask if he wanted to join us for the noon meal, he jumped inside his wagon and from behind closed doors replied, "No thank you, ma'am, I don't believe I will."

Henry Tucker lived at the heart of the ranch, although like Ben, he talked to almost no one. He was tall and Lincoln-esque, a man in his seventies who had to stoop in order to move about in his tiny, hump-backed trailer—a posture that stuck with him out-of-doors. To top off his gawkiness, he wore a dirty, narrow-brimmed Stetson. He hated women because somewhere in his roamings he'd picked up a case of syphilis. Its debilitating effects had made him "not quite right in the head." He was the one we found scolding a dead cow and saying, "I never want you to do this again." When Henry drove the front loader during lambing, everyone stayed out of his way. Once he careened down the alley between pens side-swiping panels and sheep, crashed through the east wall of the sheds, and came to a stop with a scoopful of splintered boards while lambs ran loose on the highway.

Lambing, which started in late February and ended in April, was one of the times of year when everyone on the ranch worked closely together. Sheep wagons, pulled in from their lonely sentinels on the range, were lined up behind the sun sheds. Because of the cramped quarters there were feuds. Three or four of the herders would always insist on having their wagons moved: Albert's to the far side of the small shed; Ed's in front of the cookhouse; Rudy's by the horse corral. Even in close proximity the sheepherders, who lived alone ten months of the year, remained aloof.

While there was plenty of work for everyone, some herders

preferred to "winter in town." That meant going to the bars with nine months' pay—about $2,700—and spending it as quickly as possible. When they were broke, they'd borrow from the ranch. This was the dark side of paternalism: a down-on-his luck herder quickly became an indentured servant, working all year to pay off his debts from the previous season.

With fifteen thousand sheep to lamb out the two big sheds ran twenty-four hours a day—a hospital maternity ward experiencing an epidemic. It smelled strongly of ammonia, wet straw, and wool. At the end of each alley, between rows of pens, green light from the skylights shone down on neat piles of dead lambs. Some they skinned, dressing an orphaned lamb with the hide in hopes that the ewe who had just lost her lamb would think the "jacketed" lamb was hers. Men and women from surrounding ranches and towns were hired to work in the sheds. Some did nothing but fill water troughs all day; others "picked drop"—pulled newborn lambs inside from the drop corrals; others branded lambs and ewes with bright red paint because sheep, like humans, don't know their new offspring by sight.

Dorothy, a vivacious cowgirl in her forties, ran what they called the "outlaw shed" where she matched up orphaned lambs with unwilling ewes. Having already mothered eight children herself, she was an expert at such things. Her itinerant life read like the Old Testament: tragedy, revenge, and an on-going feeling of homelessness. During the great Alaskan earthquake her husband abandoned her and the eight kids. "He'd taken the car so we just climbed the highest hill we could find and kneeled down and prayed." Later, one of the children was hit by a car and died. A second husband left her during a stint in Louisiana, but he burned the house down first. Back home in Wyoming, where her parents had staked a hard-scrabble homestead and lost it, she hired on at ranches, maintaining a reckless, horse-breaker's sense of humor, and working strenuously between crying jags.

Cliff, the auctioneer, a small, skin-and-bones man who ran the big lambing shed, was her boyfriend at the time. He'd center a cigarette between his chapped lips, then roll it from one side of his mouth to the other, humming country tunes as he gave shots and suckled weak lambs. Fancying himself a songwriter, he read *Billboard* during coffee breaks and every morning when I arrived at the sheds he'd look me squarely in the eyes and say, "Gretel, when you're looking at me you're looking at country." The next year he quit the sheep business to raise pigs.

A town idiot was hired. Balding and egg-shaped in overalls, he had a sweet, moon-shaped face and carried a leafless willow branch wherever he went. His usual job in town was to sweep the grocery store after closing. At the sheds he cleaned pens. His watery eyes seemed to see through us with uncorrupted vision. Once, when he thought no one was looking, he shoved a hand down into the sponge of wool on a ewe's back, then wiped the lanolin across his forehead in two strokes as if blessing himself. He was there the morning the freak was born: a lamb with two heads. Someone took a Polaroid of it, then the foreman cut its throats.

While a western town will accept an idiot with quiet affection, it treats sheepherders with contempt. In the hierarchy of a ranch, herders are second-class citizens. Economics is a factor: cowboys make $700 to $1,000 a month while sheepherders make only $300 to $500. Heroics and athletic prowess are

another: cowboys ride hard, rope, and wrestle calves; sheepherders tag along behind the herd at a slow pace. What their
job lacks in physical demands is made up for with patience.
Herders stay out on the range with their sheep year around;
cowboys go home at night.

Part of the sheepherder's mystique is having opted to be an
outsider. It's a first-century job with nineteenth-century ame-
nities—a traditional wagon with rounded top and a ship-
tight interior, a saddle horse, and stock dog to help get the
work done. But to have chosen a life of solitude is seen as a
sign of failure. In most cases they've abandoned the world for
less saintly reasons than spiritual transformation. More often,
it's a social defect that's kept these men at bay—women trou-
bles, alcohol, low self-esteem. Others prefer the company of
animals. But in the process of keeping their distance they may
learn what makes the natural world tick and how to stay
sane.

Because herders are thought of as misfits, they sometimes
behave that way and adopt a self-deprecatory humor to go
with the label. "You've got to be stupid, lazy, and a grouch to
herd sheep," said Red, a one-armed Texan in his seventies
who'd lost his arm between railroad cars while hopping a
freight to come north and get a ranch job. "He was born in a
town called Liberty and he took that name to heart," his
sister told me. "He didn't even finish his schooling, just quit
us one day and started roaming." He worked in a circus "pol-
ishing white horses," rode the rails, then cowboyed in Montana. Red could be a rascally drunk—he had cut off a
sheepherder's nose with the broken end of a beer bottle during an argument—but he worked sheep gently, quietly, in
slow adagios across the range, and at shipping time his lambs

were fat. No matter how long he had been out in the hills, Red had the spruced-up looks of a cowboy, not a sheepherder. He referred to faded jeans as "married men's pants" and gave them to his comrades who dressed less meticulously.

As if to remind us that sheepherders do live apart with a unique sense of time, Red refused to set his watch forward for what he called "goofy time"—daylight savings—nor would he write out a grocery list for the camp tender—even if he could (he was illiterate)—believing that a man should conduct his business in person.

Grady, a stocky, bowlegged Alabaman, picked drop at the sheds at night. He had a droll humor and after pointing out something funny—the bored way a ewe looked around as the first lamb squirted out—his wide smile seemed to encircle his whole face. He met his wife, a Massachusetts schoolteacher, while crossing a mountain highway with a band of sheep. She'd taken a picture of him and asked for his address to send copies. Their correspondence grew. Since she had been teaching in Alaska, she stopped in the Big Horns on her way home the following June and never went farther. She and Grady honeymooned in a sheep wagon, on the job.

A binge drinker, Grady's once-a-year drunks were saturnalian. He'd chase cars on Main Street, barking at the tires like a dog; he'd shoot holes in the door of his wagon—from inside—then ask how I liked his new picture window. Sometimes he begged to be locked up. This we did in a rusted iron cage that had been the town's turn-of-the-century jail, abandoned now and lying on its side in an alley. Every few hours we'd bring him an ounce of whiskey until the shakes died down. Then he'd want a bath, a shave, and a hot meal.

While most herders with drinking problems get on the

bottle only when they're in town, others stock up before going to the hills. When bringing supplies to one herder, the camp tender's truck turned over. In the mess John discovered a healthy cache of liquor in the man's belongings. "It's for the cooking," the herder contested. "Well, what kind of shittin' dish do you cook with this?" John asked as he picked up ten half gallons of vodka.

By mid-April this "togetherness" became tiresome to everyone: the long hours, the drunks, the deep cold. As soon as all the sheep had lambed out, thirteen or fourteen bands were made up with a thousand or fifteen hundred sheep in each, then shipped in beet harvest trucks to spring range. Herding can be difficult at that time of year. The grass is short and storms spray themselves into the herds like shotgun blasts. The sheep scatter. One herder woke up to find all his sheep gone and after tracing and retracing ambiguous sets of tracks, he found them ten miles away, walking single file toward the mountains.

After one virulent string of storms I went to visit Grady. His wagon was set on a gray promontory, the badlands, a solemn seascape flowing out from around him. He was still puffed up and jowly from a binge but looked gnomish with his ear-to-ear smile and his bald head shined. "If I'd known you were coming I'd have put my teeth in," he said, laughing. Then, urgently, "Talk to me . . . tell me some news . . . I haven't seen anyone for a month." But *he* did the talking: it had been cold—below zero day and night. His dog had had pups; three of them froze to the floor as they were being born and died. She had the rest inside his bedroll under which he had tucked a fifty-pound sack of potatoes and three dozen eggs to keep them from freezing. "But I've been lonelier than it's been cold, and it's been pretty damned cold."

Another herder I visited told me it was the ducks flying overhead in pairs that made him feel left out and lonesome.

By May the range brightens up. In badlands that looked so desolate as to resemble a charnel ground, wildflowers pop up, and sage exudes its musky-mint perfume. Songbirds return to the state and hang their cupped nests among the protective paddles of cactus or string them in a patch of wild rose. Mallards cruise the water holes. When their eggs hatch, ducklings swim among the noses of sheep and antelope who drink there.

John, the handsome, effeminate bachelor who managed the sheep, orchestrated the movement of thirteen bands of sheep to the mountains in late June. For two weeks they moved, peaceful armies, checkerboarded across one hundred square miles. John pulled the wagons ahead with his pickup, meeting the herders at a prearranged spot to "noon up," and again in the evening. He took care of the older herders as if they were all his grandfathers, at the same time handling their fragile psyches with aplomb. By the time a herder arrived at the wagon with his sheep, John would have lunch ready: Spam sandwiches cut into tea-party triangles, or else pancakes, bacon, and eggs.

Between June 25 and the Fourth of July the sheep moved again, this time to the tops of the mountains. I helped Fred Murdi move his sheep up what they called the "slide"—a vertiginous rockfall where the year before he had broken his leg. Fred was a Basque who had herded sheep since he was five. He was seventy-seven when I met him, stooped and bright-eyed, and from what I could see of his face beneath a thick coating of Bag Balm, he was a handsome man. Fred was one of the 14 million people who immigrated through Ellis Island on a third-class steerage ticket. He remembered the huge brick lobbies flooded with people: "All kinds of the darks and the lights, the good and the bad, and all poor like me." During the rough December passage he soothed his shipmates with Basque tunes played on a harmonium but now, almost sixty years later, he said he played only "for the sheeps."

Fred had become a hoarder. Opening the door of his sheep wagon was to risk a bombardment of junk—chains, rusty wire, gunny sacks, broken cardboard cartons—none of it usable. His living space had been reduced to a few feet. Fred slept half sitting on the floor by the door, his mattress propped against these belongings whose bulk perhaps served as ballast against so many years alone.

Fred cut a curious image on the range: he wore rags—layers of overalls, slickers, sweaters, wool shirts stitched together—topped by what looked like a Maine fisherman's rain hat. Under it all, his long underwear had been changed so infrequently, his body hair had grown into the weave.

"I've worked at this ranch since April 23, 1937, and I'm just the same as when I started. Some people, they raise up . . . get ahead. But not me! I don't have it. And you can herd the sheeps all your life and still you don't know anything. Oh, you may know a lot, but that's just the beginning."

Fred was proud of his self-discipline. He'd taught himself English, abstained from tobacco and drink, and never owned a radio. Since solitude was the peg he'd hung his life on, he saw no point in complaining about it. Besides sheep, his one enthusiasm was international politics. He seemed to inhale the whole of *U. S. News & World Report* each week, knew where every war, small and big, was being fought, and would plead for peace, he told me, if only someone could hear him.

"You know why I have no wrinkles?" he'd ask, purring the words in an accent that sounded more Scottish than Basque. "Because I have no worries. I drink the water straight . . . and I don't eat no lamb."

The next summer Fred's horse fell with him, and he cut his leg badly in the spill. Telling no one, he preferred to doctor himself with a remedy from the old country: a poultice of fresh sheep manure packed into his boot. He died of gangrene the day before his eightieth birthday.

Summer headquarters for the ranch was a roomy, high-ceilinged log cabin set at the edge of a meadow. From there John supplied the sheep camps, rising each morning at four, building a fire, ladling creek water flecked with gold into the coffeepot to boil. Once a week he'd butcher a ewe. From Fred's band he'd select "a dry," running across the hummocky grass in a confusion of a thousand sheep until he brought one to her knees with a sheephook held out straight like a spear. He'd slit her throat as deftly as a conductor slicing air to bring on a rush of music; then hang her by her hind legs to the crossbar. An irregular creek of her blood trickled past our feet. As orange evening light shone on John's face, he disrobed the ewe, then dismantled her: the hide, the guts, the liver, the heart, then the fore and hind legs quartered. A breeze fanned the acrid smell into our clothes as if to remind us later what we had done.

In all my visits to sheep camps only one herder gave me trouble. Albert, a big-boned New Mexican with a sensuous face and belly, herded in a great, treeless bowl on the northern end of the Big Horns where cornices of snow stuck to the ridge lines until late August. The nights were bone-chilling, and by morning the wildflowers were trimmed with ice. When Albert wasn't checking his sheep, he cleaned his wagon. He mopped and scrubbed and painted the rounded ceiling "azul." Another day he would go on a binge of cooking: posole, tortillas, chile verde. Once, while rolling out a tortilla he tried to kiss me. "Be pretty good, you come up here tonight. I treat you real nice." Then he'd bolster the offer with money, a Cadillac, a horse. When he'd worked for an outfit near Rock Springs, the owners brought whores to the camps. "Keep the sheepherders abroken all the time," he'd tell me. Another day I saw him work with a colt. He hummed and spoke softly to the animal. His lecherousness seemed to be only a kink in a deeply affectionate nature, and his caresses, saved up for the children he might have had, were being squandered elsewhere. That day he grabbed my hand and placed it on his swelling erection. When I pulled back he got mad and started hitting me with a broom. It scared me and I rode home. When he came to headquarters another time, I hid under the bed until he was gone.

Bob Ayers herded half a day's ride from Albert's allotment. He was a bright, bullheaded man with a hooked nose and a world-weary look in his eyes. "Gal, you're a sight for sore eyes," he'd say when I rode up; then he'd bake me a pie. Bob had wandered onto the ranch dragging a brand-new saddle behind him in a gunny sack. He'd done a stint in prison, worked as a day laborer in Salt Lake, and cowboyed before herding sheep. Bob was a workingman's man: he didn't want to own sheep, he wanted to unionize ranch labor. "Goddamn, we'd have the whole world on its knees. But how in hell are you going to get guys like us to stick together. We won't do it. We're just too damned ornery. We'd rather starve than agree on anything," he said, pushing his Scotch cap back on his head and looking out the window. "But even if we are underpaid, I'd rather herd sheep than have some flat-footed prick telling me what I can and can't do and when and how to do it."

The last time I saw Bob he was in jail for shooting six cows. "A bunch of smartass cowboys were putting their cattle in on my pasture. I warned them . . . but they kept it up. I should have shot the cowboys instead. . . ."

He had been herding near the town of Ten Sleep, where seventy-five years earlier, the Spring Creek Raid culminated thirty years of conflict between sheepherders and cattlemen. On an April morning in 1909, two ranchers and their herder, Joe Lazier, were drinking coffee in the sheep wagon. Lambing had just begun. When they stepped outside to go back to work, seven attackers shot the men in cold blood, burned the wagon, then slaughtered the entire band of sheep.

Such violence was intended to warn other sheepmen to stay away. All over Wyoming "dead lines" had been posted over which sheep could not cross; a sign at the outskirts of Jackson read: "There shall be no sheep residing in or passing through Jackson's Hole." Near Rock Springs, 150 masked men turned several thousand sheep back, then killed them and their herder.

Cattlemen resented the arrival of sheep in the state not because sheep wreck the range as was often suggested, but because the cattlemen had been here first and wanted all the public grazing land for themselves. They had already grossly overstocked the range, and newcomers of any species would not have been welcome. In Bob Ayers's mind, six dead cows represented a token revenge.

Bob and I talked all afternoon with bars between us. I told him my favorite story about a Japanese hermit, Kamo no Chomei, who had left a comfortable life and gone to the mountains. Every year he built a new hut, each one smaller than the last, until, finally, the walls were merely hinged together. When the hermit tired of a place, he folded up his house and carried it to another part of the mountain.

When the guard said it was time to go I asked Bob if he needed anything. "Yeah . . . tell the judge he'll be wasting taxpayers' money if they put an old man like me in the pen . . . and in case that doesn't work, bake me a chocolate cake— with a hacksaw in it." He laughed as the guard took him away.

All summer the Big Horns were washed with rain squalls. The lightning that accompanied these afternoon storms struck so close sparks jumped off the metal tops of the sheep wagons. The sky seemed less like something above us than a bright finial enclosing our heads. I met "Hoot" during one such storm. Lightning hit a rock in front of us, breaking it apart. "I've already been hit by lightning twice," he told me. Hoot had the shakes. During the war he suffered shellshock and still underwent agonizing bouts of fear. One spring he left his sheep wagon and walked all night. The camp tender found him ten miles from town, trembling and shouting incoherent bursts of words. He wintered that year at the VA hospital in Sheridan and the following spring returned to the ranch with a bewildered look that seemed to have taken charge of his face and never left him. He said he couldn't herd anymore. His wagon was set behind the sun sheds near town, where he spent his days reading *Oui* magazine and writing letters home to Minnesota.

John hired a couple to replace Hoot. We called them "Liz" and "Dick" after the Burtons because they fought strenuously and she fancied herself a great beauty. When John brought supplies to their camp, Liz refused to emerge until she had her makeup on: great daubs of purple eyeshadow and clownish dots of rouge. The first week they ordered a case of vanilla. "Doing a lot of baking?" John asked, though he knew they were drinking it for the alcohol. They were soon replaced by a young man so ill at ease with domestic routine that instead of washing his dishes, he tossed the dirty plates and cups behind the wagon, then ordered more.

By the end of August the sun-cured grass had faded. The lambs were shipped and this procedure took a week. Every morning at five, three semis backed up to the sorting corrals and three tiers of lambs per truck were taken away. Afterward, the crew would come to headquarters to eat. We cooked 60 eggs, 3 rashers of bacon, 120 pancakes a day, then washed the dishes in the creek.

Sterling, who had been helping John tend camp, quit and went to town. He had complained of "a bad case of the jitters" and worried that he wasn't doing a good job. Later that week he shot himself at the entrance to town. In a letter he said, "I just got to where I had to do something, couldn't sleep or sit still my damn nerves was about shot." He was a tall, string-bean man who walked like a chicken: after a few high steps he'd stop and scratch the ground with his boot as if trying to find a place to hide. His shyness was part of an old-fashioned western style. When he lived at headquarters, he'd insist on saddling my horse, and if the weather turned raw while I was riding, he'd come looking for me with an extra slicker and a flask in his saddlebag.

Sterling died a slow death because his aim had been off—probably a result of the shakes. After the bullet exited his back it continued, puncturing the rear tire of his pickup. That's how they found him—a friend stopped to tell him he had a flat. "He bled from around two in the morning until dawn," the sheriff told us on a crisp fall morning under the badly executed bronze statue of a wild horse.

In mid-September the ewes were on Little Mountain again. The hills were fawn-colored. Loping over them was like sliding over a sable coat, but late in the day, they looked benumbed. As I watched one long string of sheep climb down a close-cropped dome of grass, a Vesuvian flow of tan clouds seemed to fall like a curtain behind them. Two dark figures showed through: a black dog and a herder. "You want to go home? Let's go home," he whispered into his mare's ear. Soon they were dots too indistinct to see.

The ranch auction was a success. Piece by piece the lamb sheds and ranch yards were carted away: feed bunks, chutes, panels, graineries, wagons, even the border collies and heelers the herders hadn't claimed. Such dismantling raises questions about the demise of the West. Historians relegate the "Wild West" to a tidy twenty-year span when rangeland was un-fenced and youngsters signed on with the trail herds moving north from Texas, but the West, however disfigured, persists. Cowboys still drift from outfit to outfit, riding the rough string, calving heifers, making fifty-mile circles during fall roundup; and year around, the sheepherders—what's left of them—stay out with their sheep. But ranchers who cherish the western life and its values may also pray for oil wells in their calving pasture or a coal lease on prime grassland. Economics has pressed them into such a paradoxical stance. For years they've borrowed $100,000 for operating costs; now they can't afford the interest. Disfigurement is synonymous with the whole idea of a frontier. As soon as we lay our hands on it, the freedom we thought it represented is quickly gone.

A week after the ranch was dispersed, one-armed Red, the last of the old-time herders, died. There were empty spaces around his trailer where all the others had been pulled away. They gave him a Mormon funeral because he died in a Mormon town, though his only religion was "the bars, the mountains, and a band of woolies." Grady was there in a blue gabardine suit so old it had turned shiny. He had stuck a white carnation into his lapel and wore a short-brimmed Stetson gangster-style. His duty as pallbearer worried him: "Gretel, I still have the shakes. But if I drop old Red, he'll understand."

The funeral home was pink inside with hardware store chandeliers and overstuffed red couches on either side of metal folding chairs. Pink washed over Red's hard life and touched none of it. Three hefty Mormon women sang "Abiding Love" and "In the Garden," their voices ululating as if gulping sugar.

"Nineteen of us herders have died since I started working here," Grady said as we walked from the gravesite. The backhoe passed, lights flashing. He waved because the driver was one of Grady and Red's drinking buddies. "They don't dig them graves by hand anymore, do they?" He pulled the carnation from his lapel and threw it by the side of the road.

"I guess I'm getting pretty high up on the list." We drove to Grady's ex-wife's house and ate donuts and fudge and drank coffee. Though the demise of the ranch had been sealed that week by bankers, long before, its very heart had been picked clean.

OTHER LIVES

The ground had just thawed when I drove to Wyoming in 1976. It was night. All I could see of the state was white peaks, black sky, and the zigzag promenade of rabbits unwinding in front of the car. It's said that sudden warmth drives frost deeper into the ground before it loses its grip, as if to drive home one last tentstake of numbness before the protective canvas unfolds. That's what happened to me that year: things seemed better than they were, then took a declivitous slide before they improved.

I arrived in the town of Lovell in the early morning hours and took a room in a pink motel called the Western. The kitchenette came equipped with a coffeepot and a frying pan; there was an antiquated black phone by the bed, and the proprietor, who was asthmatic, listened in on all my calls.

I was there for Public Broadcasting to film four old sheepherders on the Big Horn Mountains from June through September. I had come alone because my partner in the project—also the man I loved—had just been told he was dying. He was not quite thirty.

Afte a month of ranch work and long hours spent at each sheep camp, John, the sheep foreman, invited me to use the spare bedroom in his trailerhouse. "Catty corner" to the bar and the Mormon church (as he described it), the trailer was set at an angle to the main and only paved street in a town so bland it might have been tipped on its side and all the life drained from it. The interior was extraordinary: crushed red velvet loveseats, gold lamps hung from what looked like anchor chain, a pink kitchen with blue rugs, an empty bookshelf, a statue of Adonis on an end table.

The grandson of the original Mormon rancher who used the homestead laws to amass 200,000 acres òf land, John is tall and long-legged with a homely-handsome face. His high cheekbones give him a startled look and he has a bachelor's hotheaded fussiness. "You wanted to come to an outfit where things was done ass-backwards, and you've come to the right place," he said. On the way to sheep camp a coyote crossed the road in front of us. "God, I don't want to shoot that dirty little sonofabitch," he said. He stopped the truck, rummaging in back of the seat for his rifle while the coyote disappeared from sight. We drove on. "Hell, I don't carry any shells anyway," he confessed a few moments later. He had once kept a pet coyote tied up in his back yard, but when he came home from school one day, the animal was gone. "Your grandfather just didn't think it looked right having a predator staked out front," his grandmother explained.

That night one of the would-be "stars" of the film stumbled into John's trailer at two in the morning drunk and on a binge. "Wake up, Hollywood," he yelled into John's bedroom, then ran outside to where his horse was tied to the door handle of a car and threw up. "Don't you get sick in there or I'll take you so far out in them hills you'll never find your way back," John said in his mock-stern voice. The more brusque he sounded, the more affectionate the message he was sending. At three-thirty the coffeepot started perking, waking us by four.

In June my crew—Joan and Nick—and I moved to John's cabin on top of the Big Horns which served as summer head-quarters for the ranch. Filming began. Every two or three days I'd drive down the mountain to phone David. His voice was raspy, but his mind was bright. He said, "All this to become a ghost." There was no aspect of dying we hadn't talked about, and now our conversations often came to a halt. Though I was content just to hear him breathing, the silences were sometimes queasy, at others, purely ironic—an emotional iron ore flecked with rust.

Born in Swansea, Wales, David had a Welshman's hard-drinking indignation, but his brilliant sardonic asides were cooled and keenly balanced by a roll-with-the-punches good-naturedness. His dark hair curled away from a sharp down-curved nose and twinkling black eyes. A minister's son, he raged against false piousness and gentility, accepting a schol-arship at Harvard only to play hockey with the French-Canadian toughs, though he read literature on the side. Once in a New York hotel room he asked me to stand naked next to him in front of a mirror. "Look at how different we are," he said as if our rushing, mutual love had hatched out of antithesis. Except for our looks, quite the opposite was true. Having corresponded long before we met, we already knew how alike we were in all ways but one: I was healthy and he was dying.

Earlier in the spring we had holed up in a windowless cabin in a forest of birch, larch, and beech. We ate raw vege-tables and drank Guinness Stout. He fed a loaf of stale bread we had found to the "pinto" mouse that crawled into our sleeping bags. Night after night we listened to my one tape of Beethoven's late quartets. Finally the batteries wore down.

David slept little and when he did drift off, searing pain awakened him. I'd massage his back and legs until morning came, continuing on into the day until my hands moved on their own and I'd lose track of where on his body they were.

Because dying prunes so much away—everything extraneous, everything that has not been squeezed into paradox—we'd often lie on the floor wordlessly, holding hands, looking at the spectacle of the other, then break into uproarious laughter that convulsed into tears. There is no joke as big as death, we agreed.

By the time David joined me in Wyoming we had stopped talking about marriage. The doctor's prognosis had vacillated: first there was hope of remission; now he said David's chances of making it were "pie in the sky." His stay was brief. "All this space reminds me of possibility, of the life you and I could have had together," he said. His pain worsened and after ten days he wanted to go home and see his children.

We stopped for a beer on the way to the airport. It was the Fourth of July. Kids were setting off firecrackers in a grainfield next to the highway. "I'm not sure what we're celebrating," David said as we held each other in the motel room, rented for an hour, while bottle rockets and "black cats" exploded in the air over us.

The film became an absurd chore. During the next month of phone calls David's voice grew thinner. The elegant, ironic torque decelerated, then dropped away. At the same time the Wyoming sky changed. Its ebullient blue depths contracted and the white bedsheets of autumn clouds pulled it flat. After fits and starts the filming came to an end. It was late September. The last night at summer headquarters I dreamed a fierce windstorm felled two trees. Three ravens circled them; they cawed and cawed.

There was, in fact, a storm: two forty-foot pines in front of John's cabin snapped in half. Attached to them was the crossbar where, for years, he had butchered mutton ewes for food. That was the day the ranch's retired foreman came to stay at the cabin. His usually well-behaved dog acted strangely: he clawed at the picture window and whined but refused to go outside. That night I slept in town. There was a phone call in the morning: Keith had been found dead on the cabin floor. When I woke John to tell him the news he was silent for a moment, then said, "The dog knew."

I made a reservation to fly east the next day. David had been experiencing massive pain and in delirium had called out for me. Another dream crowded in: There was a ferry pulling two plywood platforms. I stood on one, my mother on another. We moved toward a small island. David's young son stood on the shore holding a message. When I debarked to read it, the paper shook so violently I could decipher nothing.

In the morning I packed and was in the bathtub when David's mother called: David was dead.

I stayed in Wyoming and went to Keith's funeral instead of David's. Keith's wife, supported on either side by her children, slumped into the shape of an "S" and could not stop the flow of tears. I was dry-eyed for a while. David's presence—his "ghost"—appeared everywhere, mischievous and glinting. It felt scandalous to be alive, obscene to experience pleasure or pain. Then a wheel of emptiness turned inside me and churned there for a long time.

The tears came and lasted for two years. I traveled. One childhood friend was indulgent enough to let me stay in his Santa Fe house and lie on top of his bed while he slept under the covers. To be alone in a room at night was anathema. Windows flew open and voices yelled, "Wake up!" I'd call John at the ranch. "You still driftin'?" he'd ask. After many months he said, "One place is as good as another, you might as well come home."

When I pulled up to the trailerhouse—after a nonstop, seventeen-hour stint of driving—John was packing groceries to go to sheep camp. "You might as well come along," he said, trying to sound nonchalant. "I don't know why, but these guys have been worrying about you."

In the next weeks a handful of women befriended me. One of the myths about the West is its portrayal as "a boy's world," but the women I met—descendants of outlaws, homesteaders, ranchers, and Mormon pioneers—were as tough and capable as the men were softhearted. BobbyJo, juggling five young children and a temperamental husband, called. "Come on over and cry in my kitchen," she said until I laughed. Dorothy, a cowgirl in her forties whose parents' homestead was an overnight depot for stolen horses coming down the outlaw trail, showed up at John's one night: "Let's go honky-tonkying," she yelled through the window, but because she didn't drink and there was no place to dance, we'd go for a ride instead. "Most people don't know what it is to grow up lonely. The only friends I had growing up were desperados and the army guys going by on the train," she said. We ran our horses across the foothills of the Wild Horse Range. A stud bunch (a stallion and mares) lunged up out of a dry wash as we passed by. We came across the carcass of a horse. Its stiff hide was draped over the bones. I wanted to cut it away and wear it around my shoulders. This was how I could wear death and still be alive. "If they ever operate on our hearts they'll need a gallon of glue," Dorothy said as we rode away.

When I visited her house, two goats, a milk cow, a steer, geese, and two dogs chained to a tree greeted me. In the kitchen a Shetland pony warmed himself by the cookstove. Dorothy appeared holding a magpie. "It's for you," she said. "You can teach these guys to talk; then you won't be lonely." She told me about another Wyoming ranch woman who, having survived her husband, brought her saddle horse into the living room on winter nights for company; she suggested I do the same.

Summer brought no rain and one hailstorm. In half an hour a friend's hundred acres of alfalfa were a field of sticks. That's how I felt—stiff, weightless, exposed. I drove to town with the rancher. He ate a whole bag of sunflower seeds, laughing nervously about his loss, and the floor of his pickup looked like a parrot's cage.

By Labor Day the gray, clayish ground had cracked. Between clumps of sagebrush it looked smooth and pale as a mask. John, two rancher friends, and I went "on a party." To "go on a party" means being carbound for a couple of days and part of the fun was feeling their legs next to mine and being destinationless. We went to a bar just over the Montana line called Snuff's. Dust from the calcium plant across the road washed everything pink. I danced in the parking lot

with Rex and Chuck while John danced inside with the wall-
flowers—three obese young women in sundresses. Later we
drove on a back road to Red Lodge, Luther, and Roscoe,
handing out beers along the way to cowboys who were gathering cattle.

At one bar a woman bent a cowboy backward over the
fender of a pickup and kissed him. When she finally let him
go he dropped, mocking unconsciousness. We drove home. I
woke from a toxic snooze on someone's front lawn. The
truck we had driven was parked in the middle of a cornfield.
The horn was blaring. When I woke up again, it was gone.

My life felt flat, then euphoric, then flat again. These fluc-
tuations gained momentum like a paddlewheel: I was dry
and airy, then immersed again. Was it a lie to be here? Was I
an impostor? My city friends called and asked when I was
going to stop hiding. Wyoming hospitality was an extrava-
gant blend of dry humor and benign neglect. But I wavered.
One morning a couple in a car from New York drove by.
"Ah . . ." they must have thought, "a real cowgirl." As the car
slowed to go through town I found myself trotting behind it.
I wanted to pound on the windows and explain that I knew
every subway stop on the Seventh Avenue IRT. They
speeded up and drove on. I laughed at myself, then went
inside and wrote to a friend: "True solace is finding none,
which is to say, it is everywhere."

After a good many tequilas-and-something (that was one of
the odd liberties of the state: you could buy a mixed drink in
a "go-cup" from the drive-up window of any bar), I decided
to winter alone in a one-room log cabin on the North Fork of

the Shoshone River. I was betting against masochism in thinking that solitude might work as an antidote to solitude.

Nineteen seventy-eight turned out to be the third worst Wyoming winter on record. After an extreme of sixty below zero, the thermometer rose to ten below and the air felt balmy. One cowboy lit a fire under his pickup to thaw out the antifreeze, then drove over the Continental Divide wrapped in horse blankets because his heater fan had snapped and he had 120 horses to feed in the valley below.

Another friend's transmission froze while he was in a bar. The only gear that worked was reverse so he drove the eight miles home backward through two towns and up the hill past the hospital, waving at astonished onlookers all the way. When his wife accused him of drunkenness he said, "I just got tired of looking at things the same old way."

It was hard to know who suffered more—the livestock or the ranchers who fed and cared for them. One rancher's herd of Angus cattle started aborting spontaneously. He performed an autopsy on one of the cows. "She was just jelly inside. Everything in her had been plumb used up," he said.

Days when the temperature never rose above zero my log cabin felt like a forest pulled around me. Outside, hard wind-packed snowdrifts grew, flanking the cabin like monstrous shoulder pads. Rusty, the dog John and I quarreled over and whose custody I won, was my only companion. I played Scrabble with him every night and he won.

Ellen Cotton, who ranches alone northeast of the Big Horns, called me late one night: "I just don't think I can get this feeding done by myself. This snow is so darned deep and this old team of mine won't stand still for me when I get down to open the gates. Could you come over and help?"

The next morning, after a passing rancher towed my pickup three miles down the highway to get it started, I drove across the Basin, trying one unplowed road after another. No route would take me to Ellen's. Defeated, I returned to my solitary roost.

I had once asked Ellen how she withstood the frustrations of ranching alone. Because she is the granddaughter of Ralph Waldo Emerson, I imagined she possessed unusual reserves of hardiness. But she protested. "I don't do a very good job of it," she said modestly. "I get in these hoarding moods and get mad at myself for all the stupid things I do. Then I pick up this old kaleidoscope and give it a whirl. See, it's impossible to keep just one thing in view. It gives way to other things and they're all beautiful."

Winter scarified me. Under each cheekbone I thought I could feel claw marks and scar tissue. What can seem like a hard-shell veneer on the people here is really a necessary spirited resilience. One woman who ran a ranch by herself had trouble with a neighbor who let his cattle in on her pastures. She rode out one morning to confront him. When he laughed, she shot the hat off his head. He promptly gathered his steers and departed. "When you want that hat back, it'll be hanging over my mantel," she yelled as he loped away. When he suffered a stroke a few months later, she nursed him, though his hat still hangs over the fireplace today.

Living well here has always been the art of making do in emotional as well as material ways. Traditionally, at least, ranch life has gone against materialism and has stood for the small achievements of the human conjoined with the animal, and the simpler pleasures—like listening to the radio at night or picking out constellations. The toughness I was learning was not a martyred doggedness, a dumb heroism, but the art of accommodation. I thought: to be tough is to be fragile; to be tender is to be truly fierce.

In June I moved again—all the way across the Basin to a rambling house near a town of fifty, "including the dead ones." Though the rightness of anything had long since vanished, I had a chemical reaction to this old-fashioned ranching community. I was loved, hated, flirted with, tolerated. I fitted in. The post office, miniature-sized and adorned with deer antlers, provided a hitchrail out front. I rode my horse there every day. Mail was handed out in person by a postmaster who had a haggard, beaten look. He once stood in the middle of the road, trying to shoot a crop duster's plane out of the sky.

Across the street a gorgeous, ramshackle stone building housed the general store where the selection of undusted canned goods was spotty, and peeling green paint fell on customers like snow. The entire north end was a majestic mullioned window comparable to any in a Parisian atelier. A big copper-colored dog named Bum ruled the roost, and the proprietors, oddly mismatched, were generous and convivial. They were native anarchists, showing no interest in false appearances, orderliness, or the art of making money.

Above town on a sage-covered bench I was told a hermit lived in the low-slung house that faced the mountains. He was a painter but kept his windows covered with army blankets, afraid not of seeing but of being seen. I visited him one day. The stench inside the house was of billy goats, dead mice, and unaired emotions. He sat on the floor with his head in his hands, but his lilting, ethereal voice lightened the squalor of the rooms. His bed was a narrow plank blanketed with torn overcoats; hanging from the ceiling by a piece of barbed wire were a baseball bat and a paintbrush—icons, perhaps, of the battle he had taken up with the problems of imagination and survival.

I met Reyna and Pete, who lived in a tree-shrouded house next to the tiny cemetery. They had come north from Arizona to find ranch jobs. As soon as they moved in, a transformation took place: Reyna painted the mailbox purple, hung a canary cage from the eaves, and festooned dead tree branches with garlands of plastic flowers. Small, big-breasted, and vivacious, she told me she came from a poor family and went to work when she was twelve. "I've been everything," she said. "I've slept on the dirt floors and also in the best houses. I've eaten just beans and the best steaks. That's how I am. I know what the world is made of, and I still love all of it." She met Pete when he was working horses at a racetrack. He had a gnarled, intense handsomeness and attributed his vigor to the potion of powdered rattlesnake skin he ate every day.

After the first cold spell hit, Reyna and Pete decided to go south for the winter. She gave a party and invited the ranchers she had worked for. After they ate she played a pretaped farewell speech because she was afraid she would cry if she had to face them. "God almighty, there wasn't a dry eye in the place. I didn't know some of those old buzzards knew how to cry," one guest said. A box of Kleenex made its way ceremoniously around the room. After Pete and Reyna moved out, the owners of the house inexplicably cut all the trees down. That's how the community felt without them.

Radiating up and down the small valley were the third- and fourth-generation family ranches. When Mary Francis— "Mike"—asked me to go cowboying with her, nothing could have stopped me. Thus began an apprenticeship that continues to this day. Now in her sixties, she had grown up on one of the big cattle ranches near Kaycee. "When I told my father I wanted to ride with the men, he said, 'Okay, but you damned well better make a good hand of yourself.'" She rode and roped, doctored and held night herd, gathered, branded, and rode with the steers on the train to market. "That really caused a stir," she told me. "When one of those green-eyed wives asked about my sleeping arrangements, I told her I'd slept with all the men but I liked the horse wrangler best."

Tall, fastidious, an elegant dresser, there's nothing mannish about her. "I guess they didn't mind having a woman cowboy with them—it was kind of unusual at the time—but they damned near burst their bladders until they figured out they could hang back and I wouldn't turn to watch them."

When Mike taught me to rope I practiced all winter inside my house, where no one could see me. After I made my "debut" she was insulted if I declined any invitation to rope and gave praises when I did, no matter how many calves I missed. That's how her seamless loyalty worked: once she had taken me on as a friend, there was no turning back.

Two other women in the valley cowboyed: Laura, who had herded sheep for John, then moved to Shell, and Mary, who ranched right alongside her husband, Stan. At branding, spring roundup, and fall gathering, the four of us rode together and worked as a team.

During calving, the camaraderie grew even thicker. One night I helped Laura, Mary, and Stan perform a Caesarean. After the epidural I held the flashlight while Stan shaved the cow's side, then cut through seven layers of skin. "Why don't they put zippers on these sonsofbitches?" he asked as the calf bobbed up in a pool of liquid, then disappeared again. Holding the flank apart, we went elbow-deep in blood to pull the calf out, our hands grappling for a leg. "Okay, one, two, three—pull!" We yanked the calf straight up, then swung violently to the side and the calf came free. Breathing began. "Looks like a damned yearling," Stan said. Mary peered into the cow's gaping side. "I think I lost my wedding ring in there," she said. Stan groaned. "These cows sure are getting expensive." Laura rubbed the calf's back with straw while Stan sewed up the cow. Both patients lived.

Walking to the ranch house from the shed, we saw the Northern Lights. They looked like talcum powder fallen from a woman's face. Rouge and blue eyeshadow streaked the spires of white light which exploded, then pulsated, shaking the colors down—like lives—until they faded from sight.

During one of those early weeks in Shell a young rancher rode into my yard looking for stray cows. This wasn't an unusual occurrence, but something about him startled me. His wide blue eyes sagged at the far corners as if pulled from innocence into irony. His mouth hung open a little bit. Always, he had a canny, astonished look quickly obliterated by a white-fence-tooth-flash smile. We discussed the missing cattle and he left.

Another day we passed each other on the road and talked.

That was the day I saw a grasshopper chase a chipmunk in circles. Later in the week, at six in the morning, there was a knock on the door. I let him in. We talked at the kitchen table. When he stood up to leave he embraced me ardently, then apologized, stepped backward out the door, vaulted the fence, and sprinted up the hill to the pickup he had left idling.

He stopped by often after that, at odd times of the day. Every time before he arrived, I'd start trembling—a signal that he was in the vicinity. The same ritual ensued each time: fragmented conversation, awkward mutual clasping, troubled departures. Sometimes there were other visitors at the house but the chemical razzle-dazzle between us was trance-like and nothing interrupted our meetings.

In September we rode the mountain to check cows, fishing with a flyrod from horseback the creeks we crossed. All summer there had been the silent, whimsical archery of seeds: timothy and fescue, cottonwood puffs, the dilapidated, shingled houses of pine cones letting go of their seeds. Now his full weight on me was ursine, brooding, tender. Sexual passion became the thread between having been born and dying. For the first time the concussive pain I had been living with began to ebb. One never gets over a death, but the pain was mixed now with tonic undulations.

The next morning, at the spot where I had seen the grasshopper and chipmunk, I found the note my friend had scrawled in red dust: "Hello!" it read, as if greeting me after a long trip away from home.

ABOUT MEN

When I'm in New York but feeling lonely for Wyoming I look for the Marlboro ads in the subway. What I'm aching to see is horseflesh, the glint of a spur, a line of distant mountains, brimming creeks, and a reminder of the ranchers and cowboys I've ridden with for the last eight years. But the men I see in those posters with their stern, humorless looks remind me of no one I know here. In our hellbent earnestness to romanticize the cowboy we've ironically disesteemed his true character. If he's "strong and silent" it's because there's probably no one to talk to. If he "rides away into the sunset" it's because he's been on horseback since four in the morning moving cattle and he's trying, fifteen hours later, to get home to his family. If he's "a rugged individualist" he's also part of a team: ranch work is teamwork and even the glorified open-range cowboys of the 1880s rode up and down the Chisholm Trail in the company of twenty or thirty other riders. Instead of the macho, trigger-happy man our culture has perversely wanted him to be, the cowboy is more apt to be convivial, quirky, and softhearted. To be "tough" on a ranch has nothing to do with conquests and displays of power. More often than not, circumstances—like the colt he's riding or an unexpected blizzard—are overpowering him. It's not toughness but "toughing it out" that counts. In other words, this macho, cultural artifact the cowboy has become is simply a man who possesses resilience, patience, and an instinct for survival. "Cowboys are just like a pile of rocks—everything happens to them. They get climbed on, kicked, rained and snowed on, scuffed up by wind. Their job is 'just to take it,'" one old-timer told me.

A cowboy is someone who loves his work. Since the hours are long—ten to fifteen hours a day—and the pay is $30 he has to. What's required of him is an odd mixture of physical vigor and maternalism. His part of the beef-raising industry is to birth and nurture calves and take care of their mothers. For the most part his work is done on horseback and in a lifetime he sees and comes to know more animals than people. The iconic myth surrounding him is built on American notions of heroism: the index of a man's value as measured in physical courage. Such ideas have perverted manliness into a self-absorbed race for cheap thrills. In a rancher's world, courage has less to do with facing danger than with acting spontaneously—usually on behalf of an animal or another rider. If a cow is stuck in a boghole he throws a loop around her neck, takes his dally (a half hitch around the saddle horn), and pulls her out with horsepower. If a calf is born sick, he may take her home, warm her in front of the kitchen fire, and massage her legs until dawn. One friend, whose favorite horse was trying to swim a lake with hobbles on, dove under water and cut her legs loose with a knife, then swam her to shore, his arm around her neck lifeguard-style, and saved her from drowning. Because these incidents are usually linked to someone or something outside himself, the westerner's courage is selfless, a form of compassion.

The physical punishment that goes with cowboying is

greatly underplayed. Once fear is dispensed with, the threshold of pain rises to meet the demands of the job. When Jane Fonda asked Robert Redford (in the film *Electric Horseman*) if he was sick as he struggled to his feet one morning, he replied, "No, just bent." For once the movies had it right. The cowboys I was sitting with laughed in agreement. Cowboys are rarely complainers; they show their stoicism by laughing at themselves.

If a rancher or cowboy has been thought of as a "man's man"—laconic, hard-drinking, inscrutable—there's almost no place in which the balancing act between male and female, manliness and femininity, can be more natural. If he's gruff, handsome, and physically fit on the outside, he's androgynous at the core. Ranchers are midwives, hunters, nurturers, providers, and conservationists all at once. What we've interpreted as toughness—weathered skin, calloused hands, a squint in the eye and a growl in the voice—only masks the tenderness inside. "Now don't go telling me these lambs are cute," one rancher warned me the first day I walked into the football-field-sized lambing sheds. The next thing I knew he was holding a black lamb. "Ain't this little rat good-lookin'?"

So many of the men who came to the West were southerners—men looking for work and a new life after the Civil War—that chivalrousness and strict codes of honor were soon thought of as western traits. There were very few women in Wyoming during territorial days, so when they did arrive (some as mail-order brides from places like Philadelphia) there was a stand-offishness between the sexes and a formality that persists now. Ranchers still tip their hats and say, "Howdy, ma'am" instead of shaking hands with me.

Even young cowboys are often evasive with women. It's not that they're Jekyll and Hyde creatures—gentle with animals and rough on women—but rather, that they don't know how to bring their tenderness into the house and lack the vocabulary to express the complexity of what they feel. Dancing wildly all night becomes a metaphor for the explosive emotions pent up inside, and when these are, on occasion, released, they're so battery-charged and potent that one caress of the face or one "I love you" will peal for a long while.

The geographical vastness and the social isolation here make emotional evolution seem impossible. Those contradictions of the heart between respectability, logic, and convention on the one hand, and impulse, passion, and intuition on the other, played out wordlessly against the paradisical beauty of the West, give cowboys a wide-eyed but drawn look. Their lips pucker up, not with kisses but with immutability. They may want to break out, staying up all night with a lover just to talk, but they don't know how and can't imagine what the consequences will be. Those rare occasions when they do bare themselves result in confusion. "I feel as if I'd sprained my heart," one friend told me a month after such a meeting.

My friend Ted Hoagland wrote, "No one is as fragile as a woman but no one is as fragile as a man." For all the women here who use "fragileness" to avoid work or as a sexual ploy, there are men who try to hide theirs, all the while clinging to an adolescent dependency on women to cook their meals, wash their clothes, and keep the ranch house warm in winter. But there is true vulnerability in evidence here. Because these men work with animals, not machines or numbers, because they live outside in landscapes of torrential beauty, because they are confined to a place and a routine embellished with awesome variables, because calves die in the arms that pulled others into life, because they go to the mountains as if on a pilgrimage to find out what makes a herd of elk tick, their strength is also a softness, their toughness, a rare delicacy.

FROM A
SHEEPHERDER'S
NOTEBOOK:
THREE DAYS

When the phone rang, it was John: "Maurice just upped and quit and there ain't nobody else around, so you better get packed. I'm taking you out to herd sheep." I walked to his trailerhouse. He smoked impatiently while I gathered my belongings. "Do you know *anything* about herding sheep after all this time?" he asked playfully. "No, not really." I was serious. "Well, it's too late now. You'll just have to figure it out. And there ain't no phones up there either!"

He left me off on a ridge at five in the morning with a mare and a border collie. "Last I saw the sheep, they was headed for them hills," he said, pointing up toward a dry ruffle of badlands. "I'll pull your wagon up ahead about two miles. You'll see it. Just go up that ridge, turn left at the pink rock, then keep agoing. And don't forget to bring the damned sheep."

Morning. Sagesmell, sunsquint, birdsong, cool wind. I have no idea where I am, how to get to the nearest paved road, or how to find the sheep. There are tracks going everywhere so I follow what appear to be the most definite ones. The horse picks a path through sagebrush. I watch the dog. We walk for several miles. Nothing. Then both sets of ears prick up. The dog looks at me imploringly. The sheep are in the draw ahead.

Move them slow or fast? Which crossing at the river? Which pink rock? It's like being a first-time mother, but mother now to two thousand sheep who give me the kind of disdainful look a teenager would his parent and, with my back turned, can get into as much trouble. I control the urge to keep them neatly arranged, bunched up by the dog, and, instead, let them spread out and fill up. Grass being scarce on spring range, they scatter.

Up the valley, I encounter a slalom course of oil rigs and fenced spills I hadn't been warned about. The lambs, predictably mischievous, emerge dripping black. Freed from those obstacles, I ride ahead to find the wagon which, I admit, I'm afraid I'll never see, leaving the sheep on the good faith that they'll stay on their uphill drift toward me.

"Where are my boundaries?" I'd asked John.

"Boundaries?" He looked puzzled for a minute. "Hell, Gretel, it's all the outfit's land, thirty or forty miles in any direction. Take them anywhere they want to go."

On the next ridge I find my wagon. It's a traditional sheepherder's wagon, rounded top, tiny wood cookstove, bed across the back, built-in benches and drawers. The rubber wheels and long tongue make it portable. The camp tender pulls it (now with a pickup, earlier with teams) from camp to camp as the feed is consumed, every two weeks or so. Sheep begin appearing and graze toward me. I picket my horse. The dog runs for shade to lick his sore feet. The view from

the dutch doors of the wagon is to the southeast, down the
long slit of a valley. If I rode north, I'd be in Montana within
the day, and next week I'll begin the fifty-mile trail east to the
Big Horns.

Three days before summer solstice; except to cook and sleep I
spend every waking hour outside. Tides of weather bring the
days and take them away. Every night a bobcat visits, perched
at a discreet distance on a rock, facing me. A full moon, he-
lium-filled, cruises through clouds and is lost behind rimrock.
No paper cutout, this moon, but ripe and splendid. Then
Venus, then the North Star. Time for bed. Are the sheep
bedded down? Should I ride back to check them?

Morning. Blue air comes ringed with coyotes. The ewes
wake clearing their communal throats like old men. Lambs
shake their flop-eared heads at leaves of grass, negotiating the
blade. People have asked in the past, "What do you do out
there? Don't you get bored?" The problem seems to be something else. There's too much of everything here. I can't pace
myself to it.

Down the valley the sheep move in a frontline phalanx,
then turn suddenly in a card-stacked sequential falling, as
though they had turned themselves inside out, and resume
feeding again in whimsical processions. I think of town, of
John's trailerhouse, the clean-bitten lawn, his fanatical obses-
sion with neatness and work, his small talk with hired hands,
my eyesore stacks of books and notes covering an empty bed,
John smoking in the dark of early morning, drinking coffee,
waiting for daylight to stream in.

After eating I return to the sheep, full of queasy fears that they will have vanished and I'll be pulled off the range to face those firing-squad looks of John's as he says, "I knew you'd screw up. Just like you screw up everything." But the sheep are there. I can't stop looking at them. They're there, paralyzing the hillside with thousands of mincing feet, their bodies pressed together as they move, saucerlike, scanning the earth for a landing.

Thunderstorm. Sheep feed far up a ridge I don't want them to go over, so the dog, horse, and I hotfoot it to the top and ambush them, yelling and hooting them back down. Cleverly, the horse uses me as a windbreak when the front moves in. Lightning fades and blooms. As we descend quickly, my rein-holding arm looks to me like a blank stick. I feel numb. Numb in all this vividness. I don't seem to occupy my life fully.

Down in the valley again I send the dog "way around" to turn the sheep, but he takes the law into his own hands and chases a lamb off a cliff. She's wedged upside down in a draw on the other side of the creek. It will take twenty minutes to reach her, and the rest of the sheep have already trailed ahead. This numbness is a wrist twisting inside my throat. A lone pine tree whistles, its needles are novocaine. "In nature there are neither rewards nor punishments; there are only consequences." I can't remember who said that. I ride on.

One dead. Will she be reborn? And as what? The dog that nips lambs' heels into butchering chutes? I look back. The "dead" lamb convulses into action and scrambles up the ledge to find his mother.

Twin terrors: to be awake; to be asleep.

All day clouds hang over the Beartooth Mountains. Looking for a place out of the wind, I follow a dry streambed to a sheltered inlet. In front of me, there's something sticking straight up. It's the shell of a dead frog propped up against a rock with its legs crossed at the ankles. A cartoonist's idea of a frog relaxing, but this one's skin is paper-thin, mouth opened as if to scream. I lean close. "It's too late, you're already dead!"

Because I forgot to bring hand cream or a hat, sun targets in on me like frostbite. The dog, horse, and I move through sagebrush in unison, a fortress against wind. Sheep ticks ride my peeling skin. The dog pees, then baptizes himself at the water hole—full immersion—lapping at spitting rain. Afterward, he rolls in dust and reappears with sage twigs and rabbit brush strung up in his coat, as though in disguise—a Shakespearian dog. Above me, oil wells are ridge-top jewelry adorning the skyline with ludicrous sexual pumps. Hump, hump go the wells. Hump, hump go the drones who gather that black soup, insatiable.

We walk the fuselage of the valley. A rattlesnake passes going the other way; plenty of warning but so close to my feet I hop the rest of the day. I come upon the tin-bright litter of a former sheep camp: Spam cans flattened to the ground, their keys sticking up as if ready to open my grave.

Sun is in and out after the storm. In a long gully, the lambs gambol, charging in small brigades up one side, then the other. Ewes look on bored. When the lamb-fun peters out, the whole band comes apart in a generous spread the way sheep ranchers like them. Here and there lambs, almost as big as their mothers, kneel with a contagiously enthusiastic wiggle, bumping the bag with a goatlike butt to take a long draw of milk.

Night. Nighthawks whir. Meadowlarks throw their heads

back in one ecstatic song after another. In the wagon I find a piece of broken mirror big enough to see my face: blood drizzles from cracked lips, gnats have eaten away at my ears.

To herd sheep is to discover a new human gear somewhere between second and reverse—a slow, steady trot of keenness with no speed. There is no flab in these days. But the constant movement of sheep from water hole to water hole, from camp to camp, becomes a form of longing. But for what?

The ten other herders who work for this ranch begin to trail their sheep toward summer range in the Big Horns. They're ahead of me, though I can't see them for the curve of the earth. One-armed Red, Grady, and Ed; Bob, who always bakes a pie when he sees me riding toward his camp; Fred, wearer of rags; "Amorous Albert"; Rudy, Bertha, and Ed; and, finally, Doug, who travels circuslike with a menagerie of goats, roosters, colts, and dogs and keeps warm in the winter by sleeping with one of the nannies. A peaceful army, of which I am the tail end, moving in ragtag unison across the prairie.

A day goes by. Every shiver of grass counts. The shallows and dapples in air that give grass life are like water. The bobcat returns nightly. During easy jags of sleep the dog's dream-paws chase coyotes. I ride to the sheep. Empty sky, an absolute blue. Empty heart. Sunburned face blotches brown. Another layer of skin to peel, to meet myself again in the mirror. A plane passes overhead—probably the government trapper. I'm waving hello, but he speeds away.

Now it's tomorrow. I can hear John's truck, the stock racks speak before I can actually see him, and it's a long time shortening the distance between us.

"Hello."

"Hello."

He turns away because something tender he doesn't want me to see registers in his face.

"I'm moving you up on the bench. Take the sheep right out the tail end of this valley, then take them to water. It's where the tree is. I'll set your wagon by that road."

"What road?" I ask timidly.

Then he does look at me. He's trying to suppress a smile but speaks impatiently.

"You can see to hell and back up there, Gretel."

I ride to the sheep, but the heat of the day has already come on sizzling. It's too late to get them moving; they shade up defiantly, their heads knitted together into a wool umbrella. From the ridge there's whooping and yelling and rocks being thrown. It's John trying to get the sheep moving again. In a dust blizzard we squeeze them up the road, over a sharp lip onto the bench.

Here, there's wide-open country. A view. Sheep string out excitedly. I can see a hundred miles in every direction. When I catch up with John I get off my horse. We stand facing each other, then embrace quickly. He holds me close, then pulls away briskly and scuffles the sandy dirt with his boot.

"I've got to get back to town. Need anything?"

"Naw . . . I'm fine. Maybe a hat . . ."

He turns and walks his long-legged walk across the

benchland. In the distance, at the pickup, an empty beer can falls on the ground when he gets in. I can hear his radio as he bumps toward town. Dust rises like an evening gown behind his truck. It flies free for a moment, then returns, leisurely, to the habitual road—that bruised string which leads to and from my heart.

FRIENDS, FOES,
AND
WORKING ANIMALS

I used to walk in my sleep. On clear nights when the seals barked and played in phosphorescent waves, I climbed out the window and slept in a horse stall. Those "wild-child" stories never seemed odd to me; I had the idea that I was one of them, refusing to talk, sleeping only on the floor. Having become a city dweller, the back-to-the-land fad left me cold and I had never thought of moving to Wyoming. But here I am, and unexpectedly, my noctambulist's world has returned. Not in the sense that I still walk in my sleep—such restlessness has left me—but rather, the intimacy with what is animal in me has returned. To live and work on a ranch implicates me in new ways: I have blood on my hands and noises in my throat that aren't human.

Animals give us their constant, unjaded faces and we burden them with our bodies and civilized ordeals. We're both humbled by and imperious with them. We're comrades who save each other's lives. The horse we pulled from a boghole this morning bucked someone off later in the day; one stock dog refuses to work sheep, while another brings back a calf we had overlooked while trailing cattle to another pasture;

the heifer we doctored for pneumonia backed up to a wash and dropped her newborn calf over the edge; the horse that brings us home safely in the dark kicks us the next day. On and on it goes. What's stubborn, secretive, dumb, and keen in us bumps up against those same qualities in them. Their births and deaths are as jolting and random as ours, and because ranchers are food producers, we give ourselves as wholly to the sacrament of nurturing as to the communion of eating their flesh. What develops in this odd partnership is a stripped-down compassion, one that is made of frankness and respect and rigorously excludes sentimentality.

What makes westerners leery of "outsiders"—townspeople and city-slickers—is their patronizing attitude toward animals. "I don't know what in the hell makes those guys think they're smarter than my horse. Nothing I see them do would make me believe it," a cowboy told me. "They may like their steaks, but they sure don't want to help out when it comes to butchering. And their damned back-yard horses are spoiled. They make it hard for a horse to do something right and easy for him to do everything wrong. They're scared to get hot and tired and dirty out here like us; then they don't understand why a horse won't work for them."

On a ranch, a mother cow must produce calves, a bull has to perform, a stock dog and working horse should display ambition, savvy, and heart. If they don't, they're sold or shot. But these relationships of mutual dependency can't be dismissed so briskly. An animal's wordlessness takes on the cleansing qualities of space: we freefall through the beguiling operations of our own minds with which we calculate our miseries to responses that are immediate. Animals hold us to what is present: to who we are at the time, not who we've been or how our bank accounts describe us. What is obvious to an animal is not the embellishment that fattens our emotional résumés but what's bedrock and current in us: aggression, fear, insecurity, happiness, or equanimity. Because they have the ability to read our involuntary tics and scents, we're transparent to them and thus exposed—we're finally ourselves.

Living with animals makes us redefine our ideas about intelligence. Horses are as mischievous as they are dependable. Stupid enough to let us use them, they are cunning enough to catch us off guard. We pay for their loyalty: they can be willful, hard to catch, dangerous to shoe, and buck on frosty mornings. In turn, they'll work themselves into a lather cutting cows, not for the praise they'll get but for the simple glory of outdodging a calf or catching up with an errant steer. The outlaws in a horse herd earn their ominous names—the red roan called Bonecrusher, the sorrel gelding referred to as Widowmaker. Others are talented but insist on having things their own way. One horse used only for roping doesn't like to be tied up by the reins. As soon as you jump off he'll rub the headstall over his ears and let the bit drop from his mouth, then just stand there as if he were tied to the post. The horses that sheepherders use become chummy. They'll stick their heads into a wagon when you get the cookies out, and eat the dogfood. One sheepherder I knew, decked out in bedroom slippers and baggy pants, rode his gelding all summer with nothing but bailing string tied around the horse's neck. They picnicked together every day on the lunch the herder had fixed: two sandwiches and a can of beer for each of them.

A dog's reception of the jolts and currents of life comes in more clearly than a horse's. Ranchers use special breeds of dogs to work livestock—blue and red heelers, border collies, Australian shepherds, and kelpies. Heelers, favored by cattlemen, are small, muscular dogs with wide heads and short, blue-gray hair. Their wide and deep chests enable them— like the quarter horse—to run fast for a short distance and endow them with extra lung capacity to work at high altitudes. By instinct they move cows, not by barking at them but by nipping their heels. What's uncanny about all these breeds is their responsiveness to human beings: we don't shout commands, we whisper directions, and because of their unshakable desire to please us, they can be called back from chasing a cow instantaneously. Language is not an obstacle to these dogs; they learn words very quickly. I know several dogs who are bilingual: they understand Spanish and English. Others are whizzes with names. On a pack trip my dog learned the names of ten horses and remembered the horse and the sound of his name for years. One friend taught his cowdog to jump onto the saddle so he could see the herd ahead, wait for a command with his front feet riding the neck of the horse, then leap to the ground and bring a calf back or turn the whole herd.

My dog was born under a sheep wagon. He's a blue heeler–kelpie cross with a natural bobbed tail. Kelpies, developed in Australia in the nineteenth century, are also called dingoes, though they're part Scottish sheepdog too. While the instinct to work livestock is apparent from the time they are puppies, they benefit from further instruction, the way anyone with natural talent does. They're not sent to obedience school; these dogs learn from each other. A pup, like mine was, lives at sheep camp and is sent out with an older dog to learn his way around a band of sheep. They learn to turn the herd, to bring back strays, and to stay behind the horse when they're not needed.

Dogs who work sheep have to be gentler than cowdogs. Sheep are skittish and have a natural fear of dogs, whereas a mother cow will turn and fight a dog who gets near her calf. If kelpies, border collies, and Australian shepherds cower, they do so from timidness and because they've learned to stay low and out of sight of the sheep, With their pointed ears and handsome, wolfish faces, their resemblence to coyotes is eerie. But their instinct to work sheep is only a refinement of the desire to kill; they lick their chops as they approach the herd.

After a two-year apprenticeship at sheep camp, Rusty came home with me. He was carsick all the way, never having ridden in a vehicle, and, once home, there were more firsts: when I flushed the toilet, he ran out the door; he tried to lick the image on the screen of the television; when the phone rang he jumped on my lap, shoving his head under my arm. In April the ewes and lambs were trailed to spring range and Rusty rejoined them. By his second birthday he had walked two hundred miles behind a horse, returning to the mountain top where he had been born.

Dogs read minds and also maps. Henry III's greyhound tracked the king's coach from Switzerland to Paris, while another dog found his owner in the trenches during World War I. They anticipate comings and goings and seem to possess a prescient knowledge of danger. The night before a sheep foreman died, his usually well-behaved blue heeler acted strangely. All afternoon he scratched at the windows in an agony of panic, yet refused to go outside. The next day Keith was found dead on the kitchen floor, the dog standing over the man's chest as if shielding the defective heart that had killed his master.

While we cherish these personable working animals, we unfairly malign those that live in herds. Konrad Lorenz thinks of the anonymous flock as the first society, not unlike early medieval cities: the flock works as a wall of defense protecting the individual against aggressors. Herds are democratic, nonhierarchical. Wyoming's landscapes are so wide they can accommodate the generality of a herd. A band of fifteen hundred sheep moves across the range like a single body of water. To work them in a corral means opposing them: if you walk back through the middle of the herd, they will flow forward around you as if you were a rock in a stream. Sheep graze up a slope, not down the way cows do, as if they were curds of cream rising.

Cows are less herd-smart, less adhesive, less self-governing. On long treks, they travel single file, or in small, ambiguous crowds from which individuals veer off in a variety of directions. That's why cowboying is more arduous than herding sheep. On a long circle, cowboys are assigned positions and work like traffic cops directing the cattle. Those that "ride point" are the front men. They take charge of the herd's course, turning the lead down a draw, up a ridge line, down a creek, galloping ahead to chase off steers or bulls from someone else's herd, then quickly returning to check the speed of the long column. The cowboys at the back "ride drag." They push the cows along and pick up stragglers and defectors, inhaling the sweet and pungent perfume of the animals—a mixture of sage, sweet grass, milk, and hide, along with gulps of dust.

What we may miss in human interaction here we make up for by rubbing elbows with wild animals. Their florid, temperamental lives parallel ours, as do their imperfect societies. They fight and bicker, show off, and make love. I watched a Big Horn ram in rut chase a ewe around a tree for an hour. When he caught and mounted her, his horns hit a low branch and he fell off. She ran away with a younger ram in pursuit. The last I saw of them, she was headed for a dense thicket of willows and the old ram was peering through the maze looking for her.

When winter comes there is a sudden population drop. Frogs, prairie dogs, rattlesnakes, and rabbits go underground, while the mallards and cinnamon teal, as well as scores of songbirds, fly south because they are smarter than we are. One winter day I saw a coyote take a fawn down on our frozen lake where in summer I row through fragrant flowers. He jumped her, grabbed her hind leg, and hung on as she ran. Halfway across the lake the fawn fell and the coyote went for her jugular. In a minute she was dead. Delighted with his catch, he dragged her here and there on the ice, then lay down next to her in a loving way and rubbed his silvery ruff in her hair before he ate her.

In late spring, which here, at six thousand feet, is June, the cow elk become proud mothers. They bring their day-old calves to a hill just above the ranch so we can see them. They're spotted like fawns but larger, and because they are so young, they wobble and fall when they try to play.

Hot summer weather brings the snakes and bugs. It's said that 80 percent of all animal species are insects, including six thousand kinds of ants and ten thousand bugs that sing. Like the wild ducks that use our lake as a flyaway, insects come and go seasonally. Mosquitoes come early and stay late, followed by black flies, gnats, Stendhalian red-and-black ants, then yellow jackets and wasps.

I know it does no good to ask historical questions—why so many insects exist—so I content myself with the cold ingenuity of their lives. In winter ants excavate below their hills and live snugly in subterranean chambers. Their heating system is unique. Worker ants go above ground and act as solar collectors, descending frequently to radiate heat below. They know when spring has come because the workers signal the change of seasons with the sudden increase of body heat: it's time to reinhabit the hill.

In a drought year rattlesnakes are epidemic. I sharpen my shovel before I irrigate the alfalfa fields and harvest vegetables carrying a shotgun. Rattlesnakes have heat sensors and move toward warm things. I tried nude sunbathing once: I fell asleep and woke just in time to see the grim, flat head of a snake angling toward me. Our new stock dog wasn't as lucky. A pup, he was bitten three times in one summer. After the first bite he staggered across the hayfield toward me, then keeled over, his eyes rolling back and his body shaking. The cure for snakebite is the same for animals as it is for humans: a costly antiserum must be injected as quickly as possible. I had to carry the dog half a mile to my pickup. By the time I had driven the thirty miles to town, his head and neck had swollen to a ghoulish size, but two days later he was heeling cows again.

Fall brings the wildlife down from the mountains. Elk and deer migrate through our front yard while in the steep draws above us, mountain lions and black bears settle in for the winter. Last night, while I was sleeping on the veranda, the sound of clattering dishes turned out to be two buck deer sparring in front of my bed. Later, a porcupine and her baby waddled past: "Meeee . . . meeee . . . meeee," the mother squeaked to keep the young one trundling along. From midnight until dawn I heard the bull elk bugle—a whistling, looping squeal that sounds porpoiselike at first, and then like a charging elephant. The screaming catlike sound that wakes us every few nights is a bobcat crouched in the apple tree.

Bobcats are small, weighing only twenty pounds or so, with short tails and long, rabbity back feet. They can nurse two small litters of kittens a year. "She's meaner than a cotton sack full of wildcats," I heard a cowboy say about a woman he'd met in the bar the night before. A famous riverman's boast from the paddlewheel days on the Mississippi goes this way: "I'm all man, save what's wildcat and extra lightning." *Les chats sauvages,* the French call them, but their savagery impresses me much less than their acrobatic skills. Bobcats will kill a doe by falling on her from a tree and riding her shoulders as she runs, reaching around and scratching her face until she falls. But just as I was falling asleep again, I thought I heard the bobcat purring.

THE SMOOTH SKULL
OF WINTER

Winter looks like a fictional place, an elaborate simplicity, a Nabokovian invention of rarefied detail. Winds howl all night and day, pushing litters of storm fronts from the Beartooth to the Big Horn Mountains. When it lets up, the mountains disappear. The hayfield that runs east from my house ends in a curl of clouds that have fallen like sails luffing from sky to ground. Snow returns across the field to me, and the cows, dusted with white, look like snowcapped continents drifting.

The poet Seamus Heaney said that landscape is sacramental, to be read as text. Earth is instinct: perfect, irrational, semiotic. If I read winter right, it is a scroll—the white growing wider and wider like the sweep of an arm—and from it we gain a peripheral vision, a capacity for what Nabokov calls "those asides of spirit, those footnotes in the volume of life by which we know life and find it to be good."

Not unlike emotional transitions—the loss of a friend or the beginning of new work—the passage of seasons is often so belabored and quixotic as to deserve separate names so the year might be divided eight ways instead of four.

This fall ducks flew across the sky in great "V"s as if that one letter were defecting from the alphabet, and when the songbirds climbed to the memorized pathways that route them to winter quarters, they lifted off in a confusion, like paper scraps blown from my writing room.

A Wyoming winter laminates the earth with white, then hardens the lacquer work with wind. Storms come announced by what old-timers call "mare's tails"—long wisps that lash out from a snow cloud's body. Jack Davis, a packer who used to trail his mules all the way from Wyoming to southern Arizona when the first snows came, said, "The first snowball that hits you is God's fault; the second one is yours."

Every three days or so white pastures glide overhead and drop themselves like skeins of hair to earth. The Chinese call snow that has drifted "white jade mountains," but winter looks oceanic to me. Snow swells, drops back, and hits the hulls of our lives with a course-bending sound. Tides of white are overtaken by tides of blue, and the logs in the woodstove, like sister ships, tick toward oblivion.

On the winter solstice it is thirty-four degrees below zero and there is very little in the way of daylight. The deep ache of this audacious Arctic air is also the ache in our lives made physical. Patches of frostbite show up on our noses, toes, and ears. Skin blisters as if cold were a kind of radiation to which we've been exposed. It strips what is ornamental in us. Part of the ache we feel is also a softness growing. Our connections with neighbors—whether strong or tenuous, as lovers or friends—become too urgent to disregard. We rub the frozen toes of a stranger whose pickup has veered off the road; we open water gaps with a tamping bar and an ax; we splice a friend's frozen water pipe; we take mittens and blankets to the men who herd sheep. Twenty or thirty below makes the breath we exchange visible: all of mine for all of yours. It is the tacit way we express the intimacy no one talks about.

One of our recent winters is sure to make the history books because of not the depth of snow but, rather, the depth of cold. For a month the mercury never rose above zero and at night it was fifty below. Cows and sheep froze in place and an oil field worker who tried taking a shortcut home was found next spring two hundred yards from his back door. To say you were snowed in didn't express the problem. You were either "froze in," "froze up," or "froze out," depending on where your pickup or legs stopped working. The day I helped tend sheep camp we drove through a five-mile tunnel of snow. The herder had marked his location for us by deliberately cutting his finger and writing a big "X" on the ice with his blood.

When it's fifty below, the mercury bottoms out and jiggles there as if laughing at those of us still above ground. Once I caught myself on tiptoes, peering down into the thermometer as if there were an extension inside inscribed with higher and higher declarations of physical misery: ninety below to the power of ten and so on.

Winter sets up curious oppositions in us. Where a wall of snow can seem threatening, it also protects our staggering psyches. All this cold has an anesthetizing effect: the pulse lowers and blankets of snow induce sleep. Though the rancher's workload is lightened in winter because of the short days, the work that does need to be done requires an exhausting patience. And while earth's sudden frigidity can seem to dispossess us, the teamwork on cold nights during calving, for instance, creates a profound camaraderie—one that's laced with dark humor, an effervescent lunacy, and unexpected fits of anger and tears. To offset Wyoming's Arctic seascape, a nightly flush of Northern Lights dances above the Big Horns, irradiating winter's pallor and reminding us that even though at this time of year we veer toward our various nests and seclusions, nature expresses itself as a bright fuse, irrepressible and orgasmic.

Winter is smooth-skulled, and all our skids on black ice are cerebral. When we begin to feel cabin-feverish, the brain pistons thump against bone and mind irrupts—literally invading itself—unable to get fresh air. With the songbirds gone only scavengers are left: magpies, crows, eagles. As they pick on road-killed deer we humans are apt to practice the small cruelties on each other.

We suffer from snow blindness, selecting what we see and feel while our pain whites itself out. But where there is suffocation and self-imposed ignorance, there is also refreshment —snow on flushed cheeks and a pristine kind of thinking. All winter we skate the small ponds—places that in summer are water holes for cattle and sheep—and here a reflection of mind appears, sharp, vigilant, precise. Thoughts, bright as frostfall, skate through our brains. In winter, consciousness looks like an etching.

ON WATER

Frank Hinckley, a neighboring rancher in his seventies, would rather irrigate than ride a horse. He started spreading water on his father's hay- and grainfields when he was nine, and his long-term enthusiasm for what's thought of disdainfully by cowboys as "farmers' work" is an example of how a discipline—a daily chore—can grow into a fidelity. When I saw Frank in May he was standing in a dry irrigation ditch looking toward the mountains. The orange tarp dams, hung like curtains from ten-foot-long poles, fluttered in the wind like prayer flags. In Wyoming we are supplicants, waiting all spring for the water to come down, for the snow pack to melt and fill the creeks from which we irrigate. Fall and spring rains amount to less than eight inches a year, while above our ranches, the mountains hold their snows like a secret: no one knows when they will melt or how fast. When the water does come, it floods through the state as if the peaks were silver pitchers tipped forward by mistake. When I looked in, the ditch water had begun dripping over Frank's feet. Then we heard a sound that might have been wind in a steep patch of pines. "Jumpin' Jesus, here it comes," he said, as a head of water, brown and foamy as beer, snaked toward us. He set five dams, digging the bright edges of plastic into silt. Water filled them the way wind fattens a sail, and from three notches cut in the ditch above each dam, water coursed out over a hundred acres of hayfield. When he finished, and the beadwork wetness had spread through the grass, he lowered himself to the ditch and rubbed his face with water.

A season of irrigating here lasts four months. Twenty, thirty, or as many as two hundred dams are changed every twelve hours, ditches are repaired and head gates adjusted to match the inconsistencies of water flow. By September it's over: all but the major Wyoming rivers dry up. Running water is so seasonal it's thought of as a mark on the calendar—a vague wet spot—rather than a geographical site. In May, June, July, and August, water is the sacristy at which we kneel; it equates time going by too fast.

Waiting for water is just one of the ways Wyoming ranchers find themselves at the mercy of weather. The hay they irrigate, for example, has to be cut when it's dry but baled with a little dew on it to preserve the leaf. Three days after Frank's water came down, a storm dumped three feet of snow on his alfalfa and the creeks froze up again. His wife, "Mike," who grew up in the arid Powder River country, and I rode to the headwaters of our creeks. The elk we startled had been licking ice in a draw. A snow squall rose up from behind a bare ridge and engulfed us. We built a twig fire behind a rock to warm ourselves, then rode home. The creeks didn't thaw completely until June.

Despite the freak snow, April was the second driest in a century; in the lower elevations there had been no precipitation at all. Brisk winds forwarded thunderclouds into local skies—commuters from other states—but the streamers of rain they let down evaporated before touching us. All month farmers and ranchers burned their irrigation ditches to clear them of obstacles and weeds—optimistic that water would soon come. Shell Valley resembled a battlefield: lines of blue smoke banded every horizon and the cottonwoods that had caught fire by mistake, their outstretched branches blazing, looked human. April, the cruelest month, the month of dry storms.

Six years ago, when I lived on a large sheep ranch, a drought threatened. Every water hole on 100,000 acres of grazing land went dry. We hauled water in clumsy beet-harvest trucks forty miles to spring range, and when we emptied them into a circle of stock tanks, the sheep ran toward us. They pushed to get at the water, trampling lambs in the process, then drank it all in one collective gulp. Other Aprils have brought too much moisture in the form of deadly storms. When a ground blizzard hit one friend's herd in the flatter, eastern part of the state, he knew he had to keep his cattle drifting. If they hit a fence line and had to face the storm, snow would blow into their noses and they'd drown. "We cut wire all the way to Nebraska," he told me. During the same storm another cowboy found his cattle too late: they were buried in a draw under a fifteen-foot drift.

High water comes in June when the runoff peaks, and it's another bugaboo for the ranchers. The otherwise amiable thirty-foot-wide creeks swell and change courses so that when we cross them with livestock, the water is belly-deep or more. Cowboys in the 1800s who rode with the trail herds from Texas often worked in the big rivers on horseback for a week just to cross a thousand head of longhorn steers, losing half of them in the process. On a less-grand scale we have drownings and near drownings here each spring. When we crossed a creek this year the swift current toppled a horse and carried the rider under a log. A cowboy who happened to look back saw her head go under, dove in from horseback, and saved her. At Trapper Creek, where Owen Wister spent several summers in the 1920s and entertained Mr. Hemingway, a cloudburst slapped down on us like a black eye. Scraps of rainbow moved in vertical sweeps of rain that broke apart and disappeared behind a ridge. The creek flooded, taking out a house and a field of corn. We saw one resident walking in a flattened alfalfa field where the river had flowed briefly. "Want to go fishing?" he yelled to us as we rode by. The fish he was throwing into a white bucket were trout that had been "beached" by the flood.

Westerners are ambivalent about water because they've never seen what it can create except havoc and mud. They've never walked through a forest of wild orchids or witnessed the unfurling of five-foot-high ferns. "The only way I like my water is if there's whiskey in it," one rancher told me as we weaned calves in a driving rainstorm. That day we spent twelve hours on horseback in the rain. Despite protective layers of clothing: wool union suits, chaps, ankle-length yellow slickers, neck scarves and hats, we were drenched. Water drips off hat brims into your crotch; boots and gloves soak through. But to stay home out of the storm is deemed by some as a worse fate: "Hell, my wife had me cannin' beans for a week," one cowboy complained. "I'd rather drown like a muskrat out there."

Dryness is the common denominator in Wyoming. We're drenched more often in dust than in water; it is the scalpel and the suit of armor that make westerners what they are. Dry air presses a stockman's insides outward. The secret, inner self is worn not on the sleeve but in the skin. It's an unlubricated condition: there's not enough moisture in the air to keep the whole emotional machinery oiled and working. "What you see is what you get, but you have to learn to look to see all that's there," one young rancher told me. He was physically reckless when coming to see me or leaving. That was his way of saying he had and would miss me, and in the clean, broad sweeps of passion between us, there was no heaviness, no muddy residue. Cowboys have learned not to waste words from not having wasted water, as if verbosity would create a thirst too extreme to bear. If voices are raspy, it's because vocal cords are coated with dust. When I helped ship seven thousand head of steers one fall, the dust in the big, roomy sorting corrals churned as deeply and sensually as water. We wore scarves over our noses and mouths; the rest of our faces blackened with dirt so we looked like raccoons or coal miners. The westerner's face is stiff and dark red as jerky. It gives no clues beyond the discerning look that says, "You've been observed." Perhaps the too-early lines of aging that pull across these ranchers' necks are really cracks in a wall through which we might see the contradictory signs of their character: a complacency, a restlessness, a shy, boyish pride.

I knew a sheepherder who had the words "hard luck" tattooed across his knuckles. "That's for all the times I've been dry," he explained. "And when you've been as thirsty as I've been, you don't forget how something tastes." That's how he mapped out the big ranch he worked for: from thirst to thirst, whiskey to whiskey. To follow the water courses in Wyoming—seven rivers and a network of good-sized creeks —is to trace the history of settlement here. After a few bad winters the early ranchers quickly discovered the necessity of raising feed for livestock. Long strips of land on both sides of the creeks and rivers were grabbed up in the 1870s and '80s before Wyoming was a state. Land was cheap and relatively easy to accumulate, but control of water was crucial. The early ranches such as the Swan Land & Cattle Company, the Budd Ranch, the M-L, the Bug Ranch, and the Pitchfork took up land along the Chugwater, Green, Greybull, Big Horn, and Shoshone rivers. It was not long before feuds over water began. The old law of "full and undiminished flow" to those who owned land along a creek was changed to one that adjudicated and allocated water by the acre foot to specified pieces of land. By 1890 residents had to file claims for the right to use the water that flowed through their ranches. These rights were, and still are, awarded according to the date a ranch was established regardless of ownership changes. This solved the increasing problem of upstream-downstream disputes, enabling the first ranch established on a creek to maintain the first water right, regardless of how many newer settlements occurred upstream.

Land through which no water flowed posed another problem. Frank's father was one of the Mormon colonists sent by Brigham Young to settle and put under cultivation the arid Big Horn Basin. The twenty thousand acres they claimed were barren and waterless. To remedy this problem they dug a canal thirty-seven miles long, twenty-seven feet across, and sixteen feet deep by hand. The project took four years to complete. Along the way a huge boulder gave the canal diggers trouble: it couldn't be moved. As a last resort the Mormon men held hands around the rock and prayed. The next morning the boulder rolled out of the way.

Piousness was not always the rule. Feuds over water became venomous as the population of the state grew. Ditch riders—so called because they monitored on horseback the flow and use of water—often found themselves on the wrong end of an irrigating shovel. Frank remembers when the ditch rider in his district was hit over the head so hard by the rancher whose water he was turning off that he fell unconscious into the canal, floating on his back until he bumped into the next head gate.

With the completion of the canal, the Mormons built churches, schools, and houses communally, working in unison as if taking their cue from the water that snaked by them. "It was a socialistic sonofabitch from the beginning," Frank recalls, "a beautiful damned thing. These 'western individualists' forget how things got done around here and not so damned many years ago at that."

Frank is the opposite of the strapping, conservative western man. Sturdy, but small-boned, he has an awkward, knock-kneed gait that adds to his chronic amiability. Though he's made his life close to home, he has a natural, panoramic vision as if he had upped-periscope through the Basin's dust clouds and had a good look around. Frank's generosity runs like water: it follows the path of least resistance and, tumbling downhill, takes on a fullness so replete and indiscriminate as to sometimes appear absurd. "You can't cheat an honest man," he'll tell you and laugh at the paradox implied. His wide face and forehead indicate the breadth of his unruly fair-mindedness—one that includes not just local affections but the whole human community.

When Frank started irrigating there were no tarp dams. "We plugged up those ditches with any old thing we had— rags, bones, car parts, sod." Though he could afford to hire an irrigator now he prefers to do the work himself, and when

I'm away he turns my water as well, then mows my lawn. "Irrigating is a contemptible damned job. I've been fighting water all my life. Mother Nature is a bitter old bitch, isn't she? But we have to have that challenge. We crave it and I'll be goddamned if I know why. I feel sorry for these damned rich ranchers with their pumps and sprinkler systems and gated pipe because they're missing out on something. When I go to change my water at dawn and just before dark, it's peaceful out there, away from everybody. I love the fragrances—grass growing, wild rose on the ditch bank—and hearing the damned old birds twittering away. How can we live without that?"

Two thousand years before the Sidon Canal was built in Wyoming, the Hohokam, a people who lived in what became Arizona, used digging sticks to channel water from the Salt and Gila rivers to dry land. Theirs was the most extensive irrigation system in aboriginal North America. Water was brought thirty miles to spread over fields of corn, beans, and pumpkins—crops inherited from tribes in South and Central America. "It's a primitive damned thing," Frank said about the business of using water. "The change from a digging stick to a shovel isn't much of an evolution. Playing with water is something all kids have done, whether it's in creeks or in front of fire hydrants. Maybe that's how agriculture got started in the first place."

Romans applied their insoluble cement to waterways as if it could arrest the flux and impermanence they knew water to signify. Of the fourteen aqueducts that brought water from mountains and lakes to Rome, several are still in use today. On a Roman latifundium—their equivalent of a ranch—

they grew alfalfa, a hot-weather crop introduced by way of Persia and Greece around the fifth century B.C., and fed it to their horses as we do here. Feuds over water were common: Nero was reprimanded for bathing in the canal that carried the city's drinking water, the brothels tapped aqueducts on the sly until once the whole city went dry. The Empire's staying power began to collapse when the waterways fell into disrepair. Crops dried up and the water that had carried life to the great cities stagnated and became breeding grounds for mosquitoes until malaria, not water, flowed into the heart of Rome.

There is nothing in nature that can't be taken as a sign of both mortality and invigoration. Cascading water equates loss followed by loss, a momentum of things falling in the direction of death, then life. In Conrad's *Heart of Darkness,* the river is a redundancy flowing through rain forest, a channel of solitude, a solid thing, a trap. Hemingway's Big Two-Hearted River is the opposite: it's an accepting, restorative place. Water can stand for what is unconscious, instinctive, and sexual in us, for the creative swill in which we fish for ideas. It carries, weightlessly, the imponderable things in our lives: death and creation. We can drown in it or else stay buoyant, quench our thirst, stay alive.

In Navajo mythology, rain is the sun's sperm coming down. A Crow woman I met on a plane told me that. She wore a flowered dress, a man's wool jacket with a package of Vantages stuck in one pocket, and calf-high moccasins held together with two paper clips. "Traditional Crow think water is medicinal," she said as we flew over the Yellowstone River which runs through the tribal land where she lives. "The old tribal crier used to call out every morning for our people to drink all they could, to make water touch their bodies. 'Water is your body,' they used to say." Looking down on the seared landscape below, it wasn't difficult to understand the real and imagined potency of water. "All that would be a big death yard," she said with a sweep of her arm. That's how the drought would come: one sweep and all moisture would be banished. Bluebunch and June grass would wither. Elk and deer would trample sidehills into sand. Draws would fill up with dead horses and cows. Tucked under ledges of shale, dens of rattlesnakes would grow into city-states of snakes. The roots of trees would rise to the surface and flail through dust in search of water.

Everything in nature invites us constantly to be what we are. We are often like rivers: careless and forceful, timid and dangerous, lucid and muddied, eddying, gleaming, still. Lovers, farmers, and artists have one thing in common, at least—a fear of "dry spells," dormant periods in which we do no blooming, internal droughts only the waters of imagination and psychic release can civilize. All such matters are delicate of course. But a good irrigator knows this: too little water brings on the weeds while too much degrades the soil the way too much easy money can trivialize a person's initiative. In his journal Thoreau wrote, "A man's life should be as fresh as a river. It should be the same channel but a new water every instant."

This morning I walked the length of a narrow, dry wash. Slabs of stone, broken off in great squares, lay propped against the banks like blank mirrors. A sagebrush had drilled a hole through one of these rocks. The roots fanned out and down like hooked noses. Farther up, a quarry of red rock bore the fossilized marks of rippling water. Just yesterday, a cloudburst sent a skinny stream beneath these frozen undulations. Its passage carved the same kind of watery ridges into the sand at my feet. Even in this dry country, where internal and external droughts always threaten, water is self-registering no matter how ancient, recent, or brief.

JUST MARRIED

I met my husband at a John Wayne film festival in Cody,
Wyoming. The film series was a rare midwinter entertain-
ment to which people from all over the state came. A mutual
friend, one of the speakers at the festival, introduced us, and
the next morning when *The Man Who Shot Liberty Valance*
was shown, we sat next to each other by chance. The fact that
he cried during sad scenes in the film made me want to talk
to him so we stayed in town, had dinner together, and closed
down the bars. Here was a man who could talk books as well
as ranching, medieval history and the mountains, ideas and
mules. Like me he was a culture straddler. Ten month's later
we were married.

He had planned to propose while we were crossing Cougar
Pass—a bald, ten-thousand-foot dome—with twenty-two
head of loose horses, but a front was moving through, and in
the commotion, he forgot. Another day he loped up to me:
"Want to get hitched?" he said. Before I could respond there
was horse-trouble ahead and he loped away. To make up for
the unceremonious interruption, he serenaded me that night
with the wistful calls sandhill cranes make. A cow elk wandered into the meadow and mingled with the horses. It
snowed and in the morning a choir of coyotes howled, "Yes."

After signing for our license at the county courthouse we
were given a complimentary "Care package," a Pandora's

box of grotesqueries: Midol, Kotex, disposable razors, shaving cream, a bar of soap—a summing up, I suppose, of what in a marriage we could look forward to: blood, pain, unwanted hair, headaches, and dirt. "Hey, where's the champagne and cigars?" I asked.

We had a spur-of-the-moment winter wedding. I called my parents and asked them what they were doing the following Saturday. They had a golf game. I told them to cancel it. "Instead of waiting, we've decided to get married while the bloom is still on," I said.

It was a walk-in wedding. The road crew couldn't get the snow plowed all the way to the isolated log cabin where the ceremony was to be held. We drove as far as we could in my pickup, chaining up on the way.

In the one hushed moment before the ceremony started, Rusty, my dog, walked through the small crowd of well wishers and lay down at my feet. On his wolfish-wise face was a look that said, "What about me?" So the three of us were married that day. Afterward we skated on the small pond in front of the house and drank from open bottles of champagne stuck in the snow.

"Here's to the end of loneliness," I toasted quietly, not believing such a thing could come true. But it did and nothing prepared me for the sense of peace I felt—of love gone deep into a friendship—so for a while I took it to be a premonition of death—the deathbed calm we're supposed to feel after getting our affairs in order.

A year later while riding off a treeless mountain slope in a rainstorm I was struck by lightning. There was a white flash.

It felt as though sequins had been poured down my legs, then an electrical charge thumped me at the base of my skull as if I'd been mugged. Afterward the crown of my head itched and the bottoms of my feet arched up and burned. "I can't believe you're still alive," my husband said. The open spaces had cleansed me before. This was another kind of scouring, as when at the end of a painful appointment with the dentist he polishes your teeth.

Out across the Basin chips of light on waterponds mirrored the storm that passed us. Below was the end-of-the-road ranch my husband and I had just bought, bumped up against a nine-thousand-foot-high rockpile that looks like a Sung Dynasty painting. Set off from a series of narrow rambling hay fields which in summer are cataracts of green, is the 1913 poor-man's Victorian house—uninsulated, crudely plumbed —that is now ours.

A Texan, Billy Hunt, homesteaded the place in 1903. Before starting up the almost vertical wagon trail he had to take over the Big Horns to get there, he married the hefty barmaid in the saloon where he stopped for a beer. "She was tough as a piece of rawhide," one old-timer remembered. The ten-by-twenty cabin they built was papered with the editorial and classified pages of the day; the remnants are still visible. With a fresno and a team of horses, Hunt diverted two mountain creeks through a hundred acres of meadows cleared of sagebrush. Across the face of the mountain are the mossed-over stumps of cedar and pine trees cut down and axed into a set of corrals, sheds, gates, and hitchrails. With her first child clasped in front of the saddle, Mrs. Hunt rode over the mountains to the town of Dayton—a trip that must have taken fifteen hours—to buy supplies.

Gradually the whole drainage filled up with homesteaders. Twenty-eight children attended the one-room schoolhouse a mile down the road; there were a sawmill and blacksmith's shop, and once-a-month mail service by saddle horse or sleigh. Now the town of Cloverly is no more; only three families live at the head of the creek. Curiously, our friends in the valley think it's crazy to live in such an isolated place—thirty miles from a grocery store, seventy-five from a movie theater. When I asked one older resident what he thought, he said, "Hell almighty . . . God didn't make ranchers to live close to town. Anyway, it was a better town when you had to ride the thirty miles to it."

We moved here in February: books, tables, and a rack of clothes at one end of the stock truck, our horses tied at the back. There was a week of moonless nights but the Pleiades rose over the ridge like a piece of jewelry. Buying a ranch had sent us into spasms of soul-searching. It went against the bachelor lives we had grown used to: the bunkhouse-bedroll-barroom circuit; it meant our chronic vagrancy would come to an end. The proprietary impulse had dubious beginnings anyway—we had looked all that up before getting married: how ownership translates into possessiveness, protection into xenophobia, power into greed. Our idea was to rescue the ranch from the recent neglect it had seen.

As soon as the ground thawed we reset posts, restrung miles of barbed wire, and made the big ranch gates—hung eighty years ago between cedar posts as big around as my hips—swing again.

Above and around us steep canyons curve down in garlands of red and yellow rimrock: Pre-Cambrian, Madison, Chugwater formations, the porous parts of which have eroded into living-room-sized caves where mountain lions lounge and feast on does and snowshoe rabbits. Songbirds fly in and out of towering cottonwoods the way people throng office buildings. Mornings, a breeze fans up from the south; evenings, it reverses directions, so there is a streaming of life, a brushing back and forth like a massage. We go for walks. A friend told us the frosting of limestone that clings to the boulders we climb is all that's left of the surface of the earth a few million years ago. Some kinds of impermanence take a long time.

The seasons are a Jacob's ladder climbed by migrating elk and deer. Our ranch is one of their resting places. If I was leery about being an owner, a possessor of land, now I have to understand the ways in which the place possesses me. Mowing hayfields feels like mowing myself. I wake up mornings expecting to find my hair shorn. The pastures bend into me; the water I ushered over hard ground becomes one drink of grass. Later in the year, feeding the bales of hay we've put up is a regurgitative act: thrown down from a high stack on chill days they break open in front of the horses like loaves of hot bread.

RULES
OF THE GAME:
RODEO

Instead of honeymooning in Paris, Patagonia, or the Sahara as we had planned, my new husband and I drove through a series of blizzards to Oklahoma City. Each December the National Finals Rodeo is held in a modern, multistoried colosseum next to buildings that house banks and petroleum companies in a state whose flatness resembles a swimming pool filled not with water but with oil.

The National Finals is the "World Series of Professional Rodeo," where not only the best cowboys but also the most athletic horses and bucking stock compete. All year, rodeo cowboys have been vying for the honor to ride here. They've been to Houston, Las Vegas, Pendleton, Tucson, Cheyenne, San Francisco, Calgary; to as many as eighty rodeos in one season, sometimes making two or three on a day like the Fourth of July, and when the results are tallied up (in money won, not points) the top fifteen riders in each event are invited to Oklahoma City.

We climbed to our peanut gallery seats just as Miss Rodeo America, a lanky brunette swaddled in a lavender pantsuit, gloves, and cowboy hat, loped across the arena. There was a hush in the audience; all the hats swimming down in front of us, like buoys, steadied and turned toward the chutes. The agile, oiled voice of the announcer boomed: "Out of chute number three, Pat Linger, a young cowboy from Miles City, Montana, making his first appearance here on a little horse named Dillinger." And as fast as these words sailed across the colosseum, the first bareback horse bumped into the lights.

There's a traditional order to the four timed and three rough stock events that make up a rodeo program. Bareback riders are first, then steer wrestlers, team ropers, saddle bronc riders, barrel racers, and finally, the bull riders.

After Pat Linger came Steve Dunham, J. C. Trujillo, Mickey Young, and the defending champ, Bruce Ford on a horse named Denver. Bareback riders do just that: they ride a horse with no saddle, no halter, no rein, clutching only a handhold riveted into a girth that goes around the horse's belly. A bareback rider's loose style suggests a drunken, comic bout of lovemaking: he lies back on the horse and, with each jump and jolt, flops delightfully, like a libidinous Raggedy Andy, toes turned out, knees flexed, legs spread and pumping, back arched, the back of his hat bumping the horse's rump as if nodding, "Yes, let's do 'er again." My husband, who rode saddle broncs in amateur rodeos, explains it differently: "It's like riding a runaway bicycle down a steep hill and lying on your back; you can't see where you're going or what's going to happen next."

Now the steer wrestlers shoot out of the box on their own well-trained horses: there is a hazer on the right to keep the steer running straight, the wrestler on the left, and the steer between them. When the wrestler is neck and neck with the animal, he slides sideways out of his saddle as if he'd been stabbed in the ribs and reaches for the horns. He's airborne for a second; then his heels swing into the dirt, and with his arms around the horns, he skids to a stop, twisting the steer's head to one side so the animal loses his balance and falls to the ground. It's a fast-paced game of catch with a thousand-pound ball of horned flesh.

The team ropers are next. Most of them hail from the hilly, oak-strewn valleys of California where dally roping originated.[1] Ropers are the graceful technicians, performing their pas de deux (plus steer) with a precision that begins to resemble a larger clarity—an erudition. Header and heeler come out of the box at the same time, steer between them, but the header acts first: he ropes the horns of the steer, dallies up, turns off, and tries to position the steer for the heeler who's been tagging behind this duo, loop clasped in his armpit as if it were a hen. Then the heeler sets his generous, unsweeping loop free and double-hocks the steer. It's a complicated act which takes about six seconds. Concomitant with this speed and skill is a feminine grace: they don't clutch their stiff loop or throw it at the steer like a bag of dirty laundry the way I do, but hold it gently, delicately, as if it were a hoop of silk. One or two cranks and both arm and loop vault forward, one becoming an appendage of the other, as if the tendons and pulse that travel through the wrist had lengthened and spun forward like fishing line until the loop sails down on the twin horns, then up under the hocks like a repeated embrace that tightens at the end before it releases.

The classic event at rodeo is saddle bronc riding. The

[1] The word dally is a corruption of the Spanish *da la vuelta,* meaning to take a turn, as with a rope around the saddle horn.

young men look as serious as academicians: they perch spryly on their high-kicking mounts, their legs flicking forward and back, "charging the point," "going back to the cantle" in a rapid, staccato rhythm. When the horse is at the high point of his buck and the cowboy is stretched out, legs spurring above the horse's shoulder, rein-holding arm straight as a board in front, and free hand lifted behind, horse and man look like a propeller. Even their dismounts can look aeronautical: springing off the back of the horse, they land on their feet with a flourish—hat still on—as if they had been ejected mechanically from a burning plane long before the crash.

Barrel racing is the one women's event. Where the men are tender in their movements, as elegant as if Balanchine had been their coach, the women are prodigies of Wayne Gretsky, all speed, bully, and grit. When they charge into the arena, their hats fly off; they ride brazenly, elbows, knees, feet fluttering, and by the time they've careened around the second of three barrels, the whip they've had clenched between their teeth is passed to a hand, and on the home stretch they urge the horse to the finish line.

Calf ropers are the whiz kids of rodeo: they're expert on the horse and on the ground, and their horses are as quick-witted. The cowboy emerges from the box with a loop in his hand, a piggin' string in his mouth, coils and reins in the other, and a network of slack line strewn so thickly over horse and rider, they look as if they'd run through a tangle of kudzu before arriving in the arena. After roping the calf and jerking the slack in the rope, he jumps off the horse, sprints down the length of nylon, which the horse keeps taut, throws the calf down, and ties three legs together with the piggin' string. It's said of Roy Cooper, the defending calf-roping champion, that "even with pins and metal plates in his arm, he's known for the fastest groundwork in the business; when he springs down his rope to flank the calf, the resulting action is pure rodeo poetry." The six or seven separate movements he makes are so fluid they look like one continual unfolding.

Bull riding is last, and of all the events it's the only one truly dangerous. Bulls are difficult to ride: they're broad-backed, loose-skinned, and powerful. They don't jump bal-letically the way a horse does; they jerk and spin, and if you fall off, they'll try to gore you with a horn, kick, or trample you. Bull riders are built like the animals they ride: low to the ground and hefty. They're the tough men on the rodeo cir-cuit, and the flirts. Two of the current champs are city men: Charlie Samson is a small, shy black from Watts, and Bobby Del Vecchio, a brash Italian from the Bronx who always throws the audience a kiss after a ride with a Catskill-like showmanship not usually seen here. What a bull rider lacks in technical virtuosity—you won't see the fast spurring action of a saddle bronc rider in this event—he makes up for in personal flamboyance, and because it's a deadlier game they're playing, you can see the belligerence rise up their necks and settle into their faces as the bull starts his first spin. Besides the bull and the cowboy, there are three other men in the ring—the rodeo clowns—who aren't there to make chil-dren laugh but to divert the bull from some of his deadlier tricks, and, when the rider bucks off, jump between the two—like secret service men—to save the cowboy's life.

Rodeo, like baseball, is an American sport and has been around almost as long. While Henry Chadwick was writing his first book of rules for the fledgling ball clubs in 1858, ranch hands were paying $25 a dare to a kid who would ride five outlaw horses from the rough string in a makeshift arena of wagons and cars. The first commercial rodeo in Wyoming was held in Lander in 1895, just nineteen years after the National League was formed. Baseball was just as popular as bucking and roping contests in the West, but no one in Cooperstown, New York, was riding broncs. And that's been part of the problem. After 124 years, rodeo is still misunderstood. Unlike baseball, it's a regional sport (although they do have rodeos in New Jersey, Florida, and other eastern states); it's derived from and stands for the western way of life and the western spirit. It doesn't have the universal appeal of a sport contrived solely for the competition and winning; there is no ball bandied about between opposing players.

Rodeo is the wild child of ranch work and embodies some of what ranching is all about. Horsemanship—not gunslinging—was the pride of western men, and the chivalrous ethics they formulated, known as the western code, became the ground rules for every human game. Two great partnerships are celebrated in this Oklahoma arena: the indispensable one between man and animal that any rancher or cowboy takes on, enduring the joys and punishments of the alliance; and the one between man and man, cowboy and cowboy.

Though rodeo is an individualist's sport, it has everything to do with teamwork. The cowboy who "covers" his bronc (stays on the full eight seconds) has become a team with that animal. The cowboys' competitive feelings amongst each other are so mixed with western tact as to appear ambivalent. When Bruce Ford, the bareback rider, won a go-round he said, "The hardest part of winning this year was taking it away from one of my best friends, Mickey Young, after he'd worked so hard all year." Stan Williamson, who'd just won the steer wrestling, said, "I just drew a better steer. I didn't want Butch to get a bad one. I just got lucky, I guess."

Ranchers, when working together, can be just as diplomatic. They'll apologize if they cut in front of someone while cutting out a calf, and their thanks to each other at the end of the day has a formal sound. Like those westerners who still help each other out during branding and roundup, rodeo cowboys help each other in the chutes. A bull rider will steady the saddle bronc rider's horse, help measure out the rein or set the saddle, and a bareback rider might help the bull rider set his rigging and pull his rope. Ropers lend each other horses, as do barrel racers and steer wrestlers. This isn't a show they put on; they offer their help with the utmost goodwill and good-naturedness. Once, when a bucking horse fell over backward in the chute with my husband, his friend H.A., who rode bulls, jumped into the chute and pulled him out safely.

Another part of the "westernness" rodeo represents is the drifting cowboys do. They're on the road much of their lives the way turn-of-the-century cowboys were on the trail, but these cowboys travel in style if they can—driving pink Lincolns and new pickups with a dozen fresh shirts hanging behind the driver, and the radio on.

Some ranchers look down on the sport of rodeo; they don't want these "drugstore cowboys" getting all the attention and glory. Besides, rodeo seems to have less and less to do with real ranch work. Who ever heard of gathering cows on a bareback horse with no bridle, or climbing on a herd bull? Ranchers are generalists—they have to know how to do many things—from juggling the futures market to overhauling a tractor or curing viral scours (diarrhea) in calves—while rodeo athletes are specialists. Deep down, they probably feel envious of each other: the rancher for the praise and big money; the rodeo cowboy for the stay-at-home life among animals to which their sport only alludes.

People with no ranching background have even more difficulty with the sport. Every ride goes so fast, it's hard to see just what happened, and perhaps because of the Hollywood mythologizing of the West which distorted rather than distilled western rituals, rodeo is often considered corny, anachronistic, and cruel to animals. Quite the opposite is true. Rodeo cowboys are as sophisticated athletically as Bjorn Borg or Fernando Valenzuela. That's why they don't need to be from a ranch anymore, or to have grown up riding horses. And to undo another myth, rodeo is not cruel to animals. Compared to the arduous life of any "using horse" on a cattle or dude ranch, a bucking horse leads the life of Riley. His actual work load for an entire year, i.e., the amount of time he spends in the arena, totals approximately 4.6 minutes, and nothing done to him in the arena or out could in any way be called cruel. These animals aren't bludgeoned into bucking; they love to buck. They're bred to behave this way, they're athletes whose ability has been nurtured and encouraged. Like the cowboys who compete at the National Finals, the best bulls and horses from all the bucking strings in the country are nominated to appear in Oklahoma, winning money along with their riders to pay their own way.

The National Finals run ten nights. Every contestant rides every night, so it is easy to follow their progress and setbacks.

One evening we abandoned our rooftop seats and sat behind the chutes to watch the saddle broncs ride. Behind the chutes two cowboys are rubbing rosin—part of their staying power—behind the saddle swells and on their Easter-egg-colored chaps which are pink, blue, and light green with white fringe. Up above, standing on the chute rungs, the stock contractors direct horse traffic: "Velvet Drums" in chute #3, "Angel Sings" in #5, "Rusty" in #1. Rick Smith, Monty Henson, Bobby Berger, Brad Gjermudson, Mel Coleman, and friends climb the chutes. From where I'm sitting, it looks like a field hospital with five separate operating theaters, the cowboys, like surgeons, bent over their patients with sweaty brows and looks of concern. Horses are being haltered; cowboys are measuring out the long, braided reins, saddles are set: one cowboy pulls up on the swells again and again, repositioning his hornless saddle until it sits just right. When the chute boss nods to him and says, "Pull 'em up, boys," the ground crew tightens front and back cinches on the first horse to go, but very slowly so he won't panic in the chute as the cowboy eases himself down over the saddle, not sitting on it, just hovering there. "Okay, you're on." The chute boss nods to him again. Now he sits on the saddle, taking the rein in one hand, holding the top of the chute with the other. He flips the loose bottoms of his chaps over his shins, puts a foot in each stirrup, takes a breath, and nods. The chute gate swings open releasing a flood—not of water, but of flesh, groans, legs kicking. The horse lunges up and out in the first big jump like a wave breaking whose crest the cowboy rides, "marking out the horse," spurs well above the bronc's shoulders. In that first second under the lights, he finds what will be the rhythm of the ride. Once again he "charges the point," his legs pumping forward, then so far back his heels touch behind the cantle. For a moment he looks as though he were kneeling on air, then he's stretched out again, his whole body taut but released, free hand waving in back of his head like a palm frond, rein-holding hand thrust forward: "*En garde!*" he seems to be saying, but he's airborne; he looks like a wing that has sprouted suddenly from the horse's broad back. Eight seconds. The whistle blows. He's covered the horse. Now two gentlemen dressed in white chaps and satin shirts gallop beside the bucking horse. The cowboy hands the rein to one and grabs the waist of the other—the flank strap on the bronc has been undone, so all three horses move at a run—and the pickup man from whom the cowboy is now dangling slows almost to a stop, letting him slide to his feet on the ground.

Rick Smith from Wyoming rides, looking pale and nervous in his white shirt. He's bucked off and so are the brash Monty "Hawkeye" Henson, and Butch Knowles, and Bud Pauley, but with such grace and aplomb, there is no shame. Bobby Berger, an Oklahoma cowboy, wins the go-round with a score of 83.

By the end of the evening we're tired, but in no way as exhausted as these young men who have ridden night after night. "I've never been so sore and had so much fun in my life," one first-time bull rider exclaims breathlessly. When the performance is over we walk across the street to the chic lobby of a hotel chock full of cowboys. Wives hurry through the crowd with freshly ironed shirts for tomorrow's ride, ropers carry their rope bags with them into the coffee shop, which is now filled with contestants, eating mild midnight suppers of scrambled eggs, their numbers hanging crookedly on their backs, their faces powdered with dust, and looking at this late hour prematurely old.

We drive back to the motel, where, the first night, they'd "never heard of us" even though we'd had reservations for a month. "Hey, it's our honeymoon," I told the night clerk and showed him the white ribbons my mother had tied around our duffel bag. He looked embarrassed, then surrendered another latecomer's room.

The rodeo finals in Oklahoma may be a better place to honeymoon than Paris. All week, we've observed some important rules of the game. A good rodeo, like a good marriage, or a musical instrument when played to the pitch of perfection, becomes more than what it started out to be. It is effort transformed into effortlessness; a balance becomes grace, the way love goes deep into friendship.

In the rough stock events such as the one we watched tonight, there is no victory over the horse or bull. The point of the match is not conquest but communion: the rhythm of two beings becoming one. Rodeo is not a sport of opposition; there is no scrimmage line here. No one bears malice—neither the animals, the stock contractors, nor the contestants; no one wants to get hurt. In this match of equal talents, it is only acceptance, surrender, respect, and spiritedness that make for the midair union of cowboy and horse. Not a bad thought when starting out fresh in a marriage.

TO LIVE
IN TWO WORLDS:
CROW FAIR AND
A SUN DANCE

June. Last night, alone on the ranch, I tried to pull a calf in a
rainstorm. While attempting to hold a flashlight in one hand
and a six-foot-long winchlike contraption called a "calf
puller" in the other, I slipped in the mud and fell against the
cow's heaving flank. I yelled apologies to her over thunder so
concussive that friends at a neighboring ranch claimed "it
shook the handles loose from the coffee cups." On my feet
again, I saw rain undulate down hay meadows and three theaters of lightning making simultaneous displays: over Red
Basin's tipped-up mesas a thick root of lightning drilled
straight down; closer, wide shoals of it flashed like polished
car hoods all being lifted at once; and in the pasture where I
fumbled with a chain, trying to fasten it around the calf's
emerging front feet, lightning snapped sideways like flowered vines shot from a cannon over my shoulders. In that
cadaverous refulgence, the calf was born dead. The next
morning, clear and cool after a rainless month of hundred-
degree heat, I tightened my lariat around his hocks and, from

the rubbery, purplish afterbirth they had impaled, dragged him behind the pickup out of the pasture.

Implicated as we westeners are in this sperm, blood, and guts business of ranching, and propelled forward by steady gusts of blizzards, cold fronts, droughts, heat, and wind, there's a ceremonial feel to life on a ranch. It's raw and impulsive but the narrative thread of birth, death, chores, and seasons keeps tugging at us until we find ourselves braided inextricably into the strand. So much in American life has had a corrupting influence on our requirements for social order. We live in a culture that has lost its memory. Very little in the specific shapes and traditions of our grandparents' pasts instructs us how to live today, or tells us who we are or what demands will be made on us as members of society. The shrill estrangement some of us felt in our twenties has been replaced a decade or so later by a hangdog, collective blues. With our burgeoning careers and families, we want to join up, but it's difficult to know how or where. The changing conditions of life are no longer assimilated back into a common watering trough. Now, with our senses enlivened—because that's the only context we have to go by—we hook change onto change ad nauseam.

On a ranch, small ceremonies and private, informal rituals arise. We ride the spring pasture, pick chokecherries in August, skin out a deer in the fall, and in the enactment experience a wordless exhilaration between bouts of plain hard work. Ritual—which could entail a wedding or brushing one's teeth—goes in the direction of life. Through it we reconcile our barbed solitude with the rushing, irreducible conditions of life.

For the fifth consecutive year I helped my neighbors Stan

and Mary move their cattle through four 6,000-acre pastures. The first morning we rode out at three. A new moon grew slimmer and slimmer as light ballooned around us. I came on two burly Hereford bulls sniffing the cool breeze through the needles of a white pine, shaded even from moonlight as if the severe sexual heat of their bodies could stand no excess light. All week we moved cows, calves, and bulls across washes of ocher earth blooming with purple larkspur, down sidehills of gray shale that crumbled under our processional weight like filo pastry. Just before we reached the last gate, six hundred calves ran back; they thought their mothers, who had loped ahead, were behind them. Four of us galloped full tilt through sagebrush to get around and head off this miniature stampede, but when we did catch up, the calves spilled through us in watery cascades, back to the last pasture, where we had to start the gather all over again. This midseason roundup lasted six days. We ate together, slept, trailed cattle, and took turns bathing in the big galvanized tub at cow camp. At the end of the week, after pairing off each cow with the proper calf, then cutting them out of the herd—a job that requires impeccable teamwork and timing between rider and rider and rider and horse—we knew an intimacy had bloomed between us. It was an old closeness that disappears during other seasons, and each year, surprised afresh by the slightly erotic tint, we welcomed it back.

July. Last night from one in the morning until four, I sat in the bed of my pickup with a friend and watched meteor showers hot dance over our heads in sprays of little suns that looked like white orchids. With so many stars falling around us I wondered if daylight would come. We forget that our sun is only a star destined to someday burn out. The time scale of its transience so far exceeds our human one that our unconditional dependence on its life-giving properties feels oddly like an indiscretion about which we'd rather forget.

The recent news that astronomers have discovered a new solar system in-the-making around another sun-star has startled us out of a collective narcissism based on the assumption that we dominate the cosmic scene. Now we must make room for the possibility of new life—not without resentment and anticipation—the way young couples make room in their lives for a baby. By chance, this discovery came the same day a Kiowa friend invited me to attend a Sun Dance.

I have Indian neighbors all around me—Crow and Cheyenne to the north, Shoshone and Arapaho to the south—and though we often ranch, drink, and rodeo side by side, and dress in the same cowboy uniforms—Wrangler jeans, tall boots, wide-brimmed, high-crowned hats—there is nothing in our psyches, styles, or temperaments that is alike.

Because Christians shaped our New World culture we've had to swallow an artificial division between what's sacred and what's profane. Many westerners, like Native Americans, have made a life for themselves out in the raw wind, riding the ceremony of seasons with a fine-tuned eye and ear for where the elk herd is hidden or when in fall to bring the cattle down. They'll knock a sage hen in the head with a rock for dinner and keep their bearings in a ferocious storm as ably as any Sioux warrior, but they won't become visionaries, diviners, or healers in the process.

On a Thursday I set off at two in the morning and drove to the reservation. It was dark when I arrived and quiet. On a broad plain bordered in the west by mountains, the families of the hundred men who were pledging the dance had set up camps: each had a white canvas tipi, a wall tent, and a rectangular brush arbor in a circle around the Lodge, where for the next four days the ceremony would take place. At 5 A.M. I could still see stars, the Big Dipper suspended in the northwest as if magnified, and to the east, a wide band of what looked like blood. I sat on the ground in the dark. Awake and stirring now, some of the "dancers" filed out of the Lodge, their star quilts pulled tightly over their heads. When they lined up solemnly behind two portable johns, I thought I was seeing part of the dance. Then I had to laugh at myself but at the same time understood how the sacredness of this ceremony was located not just in the Lodge but everywhere.

Sun Dance is the holiest religious ceremony of the Plains tribes, having spread from the Cheyenne to the Sioux, Blackfoot, Gros Ventre, Assiniboine, Arapaho, Bannock, and Shoshone sometime after the year 1750. It's not "sun worship" but an inculcation of regenerative power that restores health, vitality, and harmony to the land and all tribes.

For the hundred dancers who have volunteered to dance this year (the vow obligates them to dance four times during their lives) Sun Dance is a serious and painful undertaking; called "thirsty standing," they eat no food and drink no water for four days. This year, with the hundred-degree heat we've been having, their suffering will be extreme. The ceremonies begin before dawn and often last until two or three in the morning. They must stay in the Lodge for the duration. Speaking to or making eye contact with anyone not dancing is forbidden, and it's considered a great disgrace to drop out of the dance before it is over.

Sun Dance was suppressed by the government in the 1880s, and its full revival has only been recent. Some tribes practiced the ceremony secretly, others stopped. George Horse Capture, a Gros Ventre who lives near me and has completed one Sun Dance, has had to read the same sources I have—Dorsey, Kroeber, and Peter Powell—to reeducate himself in his tradition.

"Did you sleep here last night?" an old man, one of the elders of the tribe, asked. Shrunken and hawk-nosed, he wore a blue farmer's cap and walked with a crudely carved pine cane. "No, I drove from Shell," I answered, sounding self-conscious because I seemed to be the only white person around. "Oh . . . you have a very good spirit to get up so early and come all this way. That's good . . . I'm glad you are here," he said. His round eyes narrowed and he walked away. On the other side of the shed where the big drum was kept he approached three teenage girls. "You sober?" he asked. "Yes," they replied in unison. "Good," he said. "Don't make war on anyone. If you're not drunk, there's peace." He hobbled past me again out into the parched field between the circle of tents and the Lodge. Coleman lanterns were being lighted and the tipis behind him glowed. He put both hands on top of the cane and, in a hoarse voice that carried far across the encampment, sang an Arapaho morning song: "Get up, Everyone get up . . . ," it began, followed by encouragements to face the day.

The sky had lightened; it was a shield of pink. The new moon, white when I had arrived, now looked blue. Another voice—sharp, gravelly, and less patient, boomed from the north, his song overlapping that of the first Crier's. I looked: he was a younger man but bent at the shoulders like a tree.

He paced the hard ground as he sang, and the tweed jacket he wore, which gave him a Dickensian look, hung from him and swayed in the breeze. Now I could hear two other Criers to the south and west. The four songs overlapped, died out, and started again. The men, silhouetted, looked ghostlike against the horizon, almost disembodied, as though their age and authority were entirely in the vocal cords.

First light. In the Lodge the dancers were dressing. Over gym shorts (the modern substitute for breechclouts), they pulled on long, white, sheath skirts, to which they fastened, with wide beaded belts, their dance aprons: two long panels, front and back, decorated with beads, ribbons, and various personal insignias. Every man wore beaded moccasins, leaving legs and torsos bare. Their faces, chests, arms, and the palms of their hands were painted yellow. Black lines skittered across chests, around ankles and wrists, and encircled each face. Four bundles of sage, which represents healing and breath, were tucked straight up in the apron fronts; thin braided wreaths of it were slipped onto the dancer's wrists and ankles, and a crown of sage ending in two loose sprays looked like antennae.

Light begets activity—the Lodge began filling up. It's a log arbor, forty yards across, covered with a thatchwork of brush. Its sixteen sides radiate from a great center pole of cottonwood—the whole trunk of a hundred-year-old tree whose forked top looked like antlers. A white cloth was tied with rope around the bark, and overhead, on four of the pine stringers, tribal members had hung bandanas, silk cowboy scarves, and shawls that all together form a loose, trembling hieroglyph spelling out personal requests for health and repair.

Alongside the dancers, who stood in a circle facing east, a group of older men filed in. These were the "grandfathers" (ceremonially related, not by blood) who would help the younger dancers through their four-day ordeal.

The little shed against which I had leaned in the pre-morning light opened and became an announcer's stand. From it the drum was rolled out and set up at the entrance to the Lodge.

Light begets activity begets light. The sky looked dry, white, and inflammable. Eleven drummers who, like "the grandfathers," were probably ranchers sat on metal folding chairs encircling the drum. A stream of announcements in both Arapaho and English flooded the air. Friends and relatives of the dancers lined up in front of the Lodge. I found myself in a group of Indian women. The drumming, singing, and dancing began all at once. It's not really a dance with steps but a dance of containment, a dance in place. Facing east and blowing whistles made of eagle wing bones in shrill unison, the men bounced up and down on their heels in time to the drumbeat. Series after series of songs, composed especially for Sun Dance, were chanted in high, intense voices. The ropey, repeating pulse was so strong it seemed to pull the sun up.

There were two important men at the back of the Lodge I hadn't noticed. That their faces were painted red, not yellow, signified the status of Instructor, Pledger, or Priest. The taller of the two held a hoop (the sun) with eagle feathers (the bird of day) fastened around it. The "grandfather" standing in back of him raised the hoop-holding hand and, from behind, pushed the arm up and down in a wide, swinging arc until it took flight on its own.

I felt warmth on my shoulder. As the sun topped the horizon, the dancers stretched their arms straight out, lifting them with the progress of the sun's rising. Songs pushed from the backs of the drummers' throats. The skin on the dancers' chests bounced as though from some interior tremor. When the light hit their faces, they looked as if they were made of sun.

The sunrise ceremony ended at eight. They had danced for nearly two hours and already the heat of the day was coming on. Pickups rambled through camps, children played quietly everywhere. Walking to a friend's camp, I began to understand how the wide ampleness of the Indian body stands for a spirit of accommodation. In the ceremony I had just witnessed, no one—dancer, observer, child, priest, or drummer —had called attention to himself. There was no applause, no frivolousness. Families ambled back to their camps as though returning from a baseball game. When I entered my friend's brush arbor (already a relief from the sun) and slid behind the picnic table bench she handed me the cup of coffee I'd been hoping for. "They're dancing for all of us," she said. Then we drained our cups in silence.

Though I came and went from the Sun Dance grounds (it was too hot to stand around in the direct sun) the ceremonies continued all day and most of each night. At nine the "runners" drove to the swamp to cut reeds from which they fashioned beds for the dancers. The moisture in the long, bladelike leaves helped cool the men off. At ten, special food eaten by the dancers' families was blessed in the Lodge, and this was surely to become one of the dancers' daily agonies: the smell of meat, stew, and fry bread filling the space, then being taken away. The sunrise drummers were spelled by new ones, and as the songs began again those dancers who could stood in their places and danced. Each man was required to dance a certain number of hours a day. When he was too weak or sick or reeling from hallucination, he was allowed to rest on his rush mat.

"What happens if it rains during Sun Dance?" I asked my Kiowa friend. "It doesn't," she answered curtly. By eleven, it was ninety-nine degrees. We drove west away from the grounds to the land she owned and went skinny-dipping in the river. Her brown body bobbed up and down next to my white one. Behind us a wall of colored rock rose out of the water, part of a leathery bluff that curved for miles. "That's where the color for the Sun Dance paints comes from," my friend's husband said, pointing to a cave. He'd just floated into view from around an upstream bend. With his big belly glinting, he had the complacent look of a man who lords over a houseful of women: a wife, two daughters, a young tutor for his girls. The night before, they'd thrown an anniversary party at this spot. There were tables full of Mexican food, a five-piece Mexican band whose members looked like reformed Hell's Angels, a charro with four skinny horses and a trick-riding act, two guests who arrived from the oil fields by helicopter, and a mutual friend who's Jewish and a Harvard professor who popped bikini-clad out of a giant plywood cake.

The men in the Rabbit Lodge danced as late as the partygoers. The next morning when I arrived at four-thirty the old man with the cane walked directly to me. "Where's your coat? Aren't you cold?" he asked gruffly, though I knew he was welcoming me. The dancers spit bile and shuffled back and forth between the johns and the Lodge. A friend had asked one of them how he prepared for Sun Dance. He replied, "I don't. There's no way to prepare for pain." As the dancers began to look more frail, the singing became raucous. The astounding volume, quick rises in pitch, and forays into falsetto had an enlivening effect on all of us. Now it was the drummers who made the dancers make the sun rise.

Noon. In the hottest midday sun the dancers were brought out in front of the Lodge to be washed and freshly painted. The grandfathers dipped soft little brooms of sage in water and swabbed the men down; they weren't allowed to drink. Their families gathered around and watched while the dancers held their gaze to the ground. I couldn't bring myself to stand close. It seemed a violation of privacy. It wasn't nudity that rendered the scene so intimate (they still had their gym shorts on), but the thirst. Behind me, someone joked about dancing for rain instead of sun.

I was wrong about the bathing scene. Now the desolation of it struck me as beautiful. All afternoon the men danced in the heat—two, eight, or twenty of them at a time. In air so dry and with their juices squeezed out, the bouncing looked weightless, their bodies thin and brittle as shells. It wasn't the pain of the sacrifice they were making that counted but the emptiness to which they were surrendering themselves. It was an old ritual: separation, initiation, return. They'd left their jobs and families to dance. They were facing physical pain and psychological transformation. Surely, the sun seared away preoccupation and pettiness. They would return changed. Here, I was in the presence of a collective hero. I searched their faces and found no martyrs, no dramatists, no antiheroes either. They seemed to pool their pain and offer it back to us, dancing not for our sins but to ignite our hearts.

Evening. There were many more spectators tonight. Young Indian women cradling babies moved to the front of the Lodge. They rocked them in time with the drums and all evening not one child cried. Currents of heat rose from the ground; in fact, everything seemed to be rising: bone whistles, arms, stars, penises, the yeast in the fry bread, the smell of sage. My breasts felt full. The running joke in camp was about "Sun Dance Babies." Surely the expansive mood in the air settled over the tipis at night, but there was more to it than that. Among some tribes a "Sacred Woman" is involved in the ceremony. The sun is a "man power" symbol. When she offers herself to the priest, their union represents the rebirth of the land, water, and people. If by chance a child is conceived, he or she is treated with special reverence for a lifetime.

Dawn. This morning I fainted. The skinny young man dancing in front of me appeared to be cringing in pain. Another dancer's face had been painted green. I'm not saying they made me faint—maybe I fainted for them. With little ado, the women behind me picked me up. Revived and feeling foolish, I stood through to the end. "They say white people don't have the constitution to go without water for so many days," a white friend commented later. It sounded like a racist remark to me. She'd once been offered a chance to fast with a medicine man and refused. "I think it has more to do with one's concepts of hope and fear," I mumbled as she walked through the field to her car.

Afternoon. At five, only two dancers were standing. Because of the heat, the smell of urine had mixed with the sage.

Later in the evening I stood next to two teenage boys from Oklahoma. Not realizing I was old enough to be their mother, they flirted with me, then undercut the dares with cruelty. "My grandmother hates white tourists," the one who had been eyeing my chest said to me. "You're missing the point of this ceremony," I said to him. "And racism isn't a good thing anywhere." They walked away, but later, when I bumped into them, they smiled apologetically.

When I had coffee in a friend's brush arbor during a break in the dancing, the dancer's wife looked worried. "He looks like death warmed over," she said. A young man with black braids that reached his belt buckle was dangling a baby on each knee; I've never seen men so gentle and at ease with children. A fresh breeze fanned us. The round-the-clock rhythm of drumbeats and dancing made day and night seem the same. Sleeping became interchangeable with waiting, until, finally, there was no difference between the two.

Sunday. Two American flags were raised over the Lodge today—both had been owned by war veterans. The dance apron of a man near me had U.S. Navy insignias sewn into the corners. Here was a war hero, but he'd earned his medal far from home. Now the ritual of separation, initiation, and return performed in Vietnam, outside the context of community, changes into separation, benumbment, and exile.

Throughout the afternoon's dancing there was a Give-Away, an Indian tradition to honor friends, relatives, and admirers with a formal exchange of gifts. In front of the announcer's stand there was a table chock-full of food and another stacked high with Pendleton blankets, shawls, and beadwork. The loudspeaker overwhelmed the drumming until all the gifts were dispersed. Pickups streamed through the camps and a layer of dust muted the hard brightness of the day. After his first Sun Dance one old man told me he had given nearly everything he owned away: horse, wagons, clothes, winter blankets. "But it all comes back," he said, as if the day and night rhythm of this ceremony stood for a bigger tidal cadence as well.

Evening. They've taken the brush away from the far side of the Lodge. Now the dancers face west. All hundred men, freshly painted with a wild dappling of dots, stripes, and crooked lines, bounced up and down vigorously and in short strokes waved eagle fans in front of their bodies as if to clear away any tiredness there.

When I asked why the Sun Dance ended at night, my friend said, "So the sun will remember to make a complete circle, and so we'll always have night and day." The sun drained from the dancers' faces and sank into a rack of thunderclouds over the mountains. Every movement coming from the Lodge converged into a single trajectory, a big "V" like a flock of birds migrating toward me. This is how ritual speaks with no words. The dancing and whistling surged; each time a crescendo felt near, it ebbed. In the southwest, the first evening star appeared, and the drumming and singing, which had begun to feel like a hard dome over my head, stopped.

Amid cries of relief and some clapping I heard hoarse expulsions of air coming from dancers, like whales breaching after being under water too long. They rushed forward to the front of the Lodge, throwing off the sage bracelets and crowns, knelt down in turn by wooden bowls of chokecherry juice, and drank their first liquid in four days.

The family standing next to me approached the Lodge cautiously. "There he is," I heard the mother say. They walked toward the dancer, a big, lumbering man in his thirties whose waist, where rolls of fat had been, now looked concave. The man's wife and father slid their arms around his back, while his mother stood in front and took a good look at him. He gave her the first drink of sweet water from his bowl. "I tried to be there as much as possible today. Did you see me?" his wife asked. He nodded and smiled. Some of the young children had rushed into the Lodge and were swinging the flattened reeds that had been the dancers' beds around and around in the air. One of the drummers, an energetic man with an eccentric, husky voice, walked up to a group of us and started shaking our hands. He didn't know us but it didn't matter. "I'm awfully glad you're here," he kept saying, then walked away laughing ecstatically. The dancer I had been watching was having trouble staying on his feet. He stumbled badly. A friend said he worked for Amoco and tomorrow he'd be back in the oil fields. Still supporting him with their arms, his family helped him toward their brush arbor, now lit with oil lamps, where he would vomit, then feast.

It's late August. Wind swings down the hay meadows from high cornices of rimrock above the ranch like guffaws of laughter. Since Sun Dance several images recur: the shaded, shell-like bodies of the dancers getting smaller and smaller; the heated, expanding spectators surrounding them. At the point of friction, a generosity occurs. The transition to autumn is a ritual like that: heat and cold alternate in a staccato rhythm. The magnetizing force of summer reverses itself so that every airplane flying over me seems to be going away. Heat lightning washes over and under clouds until their coolness drops down to us and then flotillas of storms bound through as though riding the sprung legs of a deer. I feel both emptied and brimming over.

A week later. I'm camped on a hill next to an anthropologist and his wife. He's Indian, she's white, and they drove here on what he calls his "iron pony"—a motorcycle—to attend Crow Fair. "You see I had to marry one of these skinny white women so we could both fit here," he explained as they squeezed onto the seat. He was as round and cheerful as the chrome gas tank his belly rested on. Surrounding us were the rolling grasslands that make up the middle Yellowstone Valley, site of the summer councils held by the warring Crow, Sioux, Blackfoot, and Cheyenne. The Wolf Mountains to the south step up into pitched rises, crowned with jack pines. The dark creases in the hills are dry washes, now blackened with such an abundance of ripe chokecherries they look clotted with blood. On a knob nearby, recently singed with fire, is Custer's battlefield. "If there was any yellow hair left on that sonofabith, it's gone now," a Crow friend who had fought the fire said. The Crows, of course, were the ones scouting for Custer, but it seems to have been a temporary alliance, having more to do with their animosity toward other tribes than a love for any white man.

Crow Fair is a five-day country fair—Indian style. It's different from ours because their roots are nomadic, not agricultural. Instead of the horse pulls, steer judging, and cake stands, they have all-night sessions of Indian dancing, a traditional dress parade, and a lengthy rodeo augmented by horse racing and betting. Looking down from the hill where I pitched our borrowed tent, the encampment of well over five hundred tipis could have been a summer council at the turn of the nineteenth century except for the pickups, loudspeakers, and the ubiquitous aluminum folding chairs. Inside the sprawl of tipis, tents, and arbors was a circle of concession stands, at the center of which stood the big open-air dance arbor.

My young friend Ursula, who was visiting from Cambridge, asked if these Indians lived here all the time. Indians don't, of course, still live in tipis, but the encampment looked so well-worn and amiable she wasn't wrong in thinking so. Part of the "wholeness" of traditional Indian life that the tipi and circular dance arbor signify is the togetherness at these powwows. Indians don't go home at night; they camp out where the action is, en masse, whole extended families and clans spanning several generations. It's a tradition with them the way sending our kids to summer camp is with us.

Two days before the fair started, the pickups began to roll in with tipi poles slung over the tailgates. Brush was cut, canvas unrolled, and in twelve hours a village had been made. Tipis and tents, reserved mainly for sleeping, were often as plush as an Arab's. Inside were wall-to-wall rugs, hanging lanterns, and ceremonial drums. Outdoor kitchens were arranged under canvas flies or inside a shady brush arbor with packing crates turned on end for shelves, and long picnic tables were loaded with food. With barely any elbow room between camps, even feuding tribes took on a congenial air, their children banding together and roving freely.

At the morning parade you could see the splendors of traditional beadwork, elk tooth shirts, buckskin dresses, and beaded moccasins, but what interested me more were the contradictions: the Sioux boy in warrior dress riding the hood of a Corvette; vans with smokey windows covered with star quilts and baskets; the roar of new wave music coming from the cars. John Whiteman, the last surviving Custer scout, rode on the back of a big ton truck with his tiny wife, who had hoisted up a brown-and-white-striped umbrella to shade herself from the sun. They were both, someone said, well past 110 years old.

Ursula and I were the first ones at the rodeo because everyone else seemed to know it would start late. The young, cigar-smoking man who sold us our tickets turned out to be an Eskimo from Barrow, Alaska. He'd come south to live with what he called "these mean Plains Indians."

The Crow crossed into this valley in the late 1700s and fought off the Shoshone to claim territory that spread between the Big Horns, the Badlands, and the Wind River Mountains. Trappers, like Osborne Russell, who hunted right along with them, described the Crow as tall, insolent, and haughty, but submissive when cornered. Russell met one chief who had hair eleven feet long, and said their beadwork was "excessively gaudy." The Crows were so pinched geographically by raiding Sioux and Blackfeet they adopted a militaristic style, still evident in the way they zipped around camp in police cars with "Executive Security Force" emblazoned on the doors. Endowed with a natural horse-handling ability, they became famous horse thieves.

The rodeo got under way after an off-key rendition of "God Bless America" (instead of the national anthem). A local band, aptly named "The Warriors," warmed up on the stand in front of us. While the rough stock was run into the bucking chutes they played "He's Just a Coca-Cola Cowboy." As testimony to their enthusiasm for horses, the rodeo, usually a two- or three-hour affair, lasted seven hours.

Before the all-night session of dancing began we made the

circuit of concession stands. Between the corn dogs and Indian tacos—fry bread topped with beans and hot sauce—was
an aisle of video games. Between the menudo and the caramel
apples were two gambling tents—one for bingo, the other for
poker. You could eat corn barbecued in the husk Navajo style
and a hunk of Taos bread, or gulp down a buffalo burger and
a Coke, the one cooked by a Navajo from Shiprock, the other
by an Ogalalla Sioux. Ursula had her ears pierced and bought
a pair of opalescent earrings; I bought a T-shirt with the
words "Crow Fair" across the front, and around and around
we went until the dancing began.

Dark. Instead of the tamping, rigid, narcotic bounce of Sun
Dance that seemed to set into motion a chronic tremor, one
that radiated out of the Lodge to knock against our legbones
and temples, the dances at Crow Fair were show-offish and
glittering. These Society, War, Animal, and Contest Dances
served no direct purpose these days, the way some religious
dances do. "What you're seeing out there is a lot of dyed
turkey feathers and plastic elk teeth, and kids doing the Indian disco," a friend commented. He's an Italian from Saint
Louis who married a Kiowa woman when he was sixteen and
together they moved to Wyoming to live with the Shoshone.
Incongruity delights him as much as tradition. "We assimi-
late a little this way, and a little that way. Life is only
mutation."

The dance arbor was lit by mercury vapor lamps hung
from one forty-foot power pole at the center—no bonfires or
Coleman lanterns here. The ceremonies started with a long
prayer in English during which a Crow child in front of me
shot off a toy gun, aiming first at the preacher, then at himself, then at me. Six separate drum groups set up around the

periphery with names like Night Hawks, Whistling Elk, Plenty Coups, Magpie, and Salt Lake Crows. Although participants had come from a great number of tribes— Assiniboine, Apache and Shoshone, Sioux, Kiowa, and Arapaho—what we saw was only Plains-Indian dancing. Performed in a clockwise motion, as if following the sun, the dancers moved in long lines like spokes on a wheel. Anyone could dance, and it seemed at times as if everyone did. Families crowded in around the dance space with their folding chairs and Pendleton blankets—babies and grandmothers, boys and fathers, mothers and daughters, all dressed fit to kill. The long succession of dances began: Girls' Fancy Shawl, Boys' Traditional, Fast and Slow War Dance, a Hoop Dance, a Hot Dance, and a Grass Dance. Intertribal dances— open to anyone—alternated with contest dances that were judged. Participants wore Coors numbers pinned to their backs the way bronc riders do. The costumes were elaborate. There were feathers dyed magenta and lime green, then fluffed at the tips; great feather bustles attached to every backside; and long straps of sleighbells running from ankles to hips. The Hot Dancers wore porcupine-hair roaches on their heads, the War Dancers carried straight and crooked lances, the Society Dancers wore wolf heads with little pointed ears, and the women in fringed buckskin dresses carried elegant eagle fans. One young man, who seemed to be a loner, had painted black stripes across his face and chest so thickly the paint ran together into a blackface. Later, we discovered he was white. A good many white people danced every night. One couple had flown in from Germany; they were Hot Dance aficionados, and when I tried to talk to them I found out they spoke only German and Crow. A blond boy of ten said he had driven north from Arizona with his adopted Apache parents. After eating a cheesy, dripping box of nachos, he went out to win his contest.

I squeezed through the delicious congestion of bodies, feathers brushing my cheeks, and circled under the eaves of the arbor. One boy, who couldn't have been older than three, in war bonnet and bells, shuffled out into the dance circle. The Mylar balloon tied to his hand was shaped like a fish. Four boys dancing near the power pole crouched low, jerking their heads and shoulders in the Prairie Chicken Dance. The Fast Dancers spun by, like wheels of fireworks, orbiting at twice the speed of the others.

Outside the arbor was a residual flux: crowds of Indian teenagers ambled past the bright concession stands, behind which a ribbon of headlights streamed, and behind them glowed rows of tents and tipis.

The arbor closed at 3 A.M., and we walked up our hill and went to bed. A couple of drunks stumbled by. "Hey. What's this? A tombstone?" one of them said as he kicked the tent. When no one answered, he disappeared in the brush. Later, the 49ers, a roving group of singers, began their encampment serenade. They sang until dawn every night of the fair so that even sleep, accompanied by their drumbeats, felt like a kind of dancing.

Crow Fair days are hot; Crow Fair nights are cold. A rumbling truck woke me. It was the septic tank man (he was white) pumping the outhouses. Some Livingston, Montana, friends who had arrived late were scattered around on the ground in sleeping bags. I brushed my teeth with water I'd brought for the radiator. The dance arbor, abandoned and dreary at midday, was getting a facelift from a cleanup crew.

All the action was elsewhere: when I walked toward the bluffs behind the camp, I discovered two hundred children splashing in the Little Big Horn River.

That afternoon I visited Gary Johnson's camp. He's a bright, sly Crow drummer. Over some beadwork repairs he was swatting flies. "You killed our buffalo, I'll kill your flies," he said with a sardonic grin as I pulled up a chair. A small boy had taken Gary's drumstick and had beaten the metal top of a beer cooler until it was covered with dents. "Let him play, let him play," Gary admonished the boy's mother. "That's how we learn to make music." To be a drummer is to be a singer too, the voice used as percussively as the drum is musically. "I'd like to steal this boy. He and I would sing every night."

Every turn of the nomadic Crow life was once marked by movement and music. There were dances to celebrate birth, puberty, marriage, or death. There were healing dances and hunters' dances and contrary dances, in which all movement was done in reverse. There were dances to count coup, welcome strangers, honor guests, to cement alliances and feuds. Songs weren't composed but received whole from animals, plants, or storms. Antelope gave mothers lullabies, thunder and wind gave medicine songs, bears taught hunting songs.

Carlos Castaneda gave us talking bushes, but few of us realized how common these transmissions had become in aboriginal America. When I asked Gary about his pink-and-red-striped tipi—the only one of its kind in camp—he explained: "That's a medicine tipi. Somehow I inherited it. The creek water rose up and told the guy living in it to dress and live like a woman. That was to be his medicine. So he became a *berdache* [a transvestite]." He gave me a serious look. "I'll do anything in that tipi, but I'll be damned if I'm going to sleep in it."

D. H. Lawrence described the Apache ceremonies he saw as "the feet of birds treading a dance" and claimed the music awakened in him "new root-griefs, old root-richnesses." In the next three nights I saw the quick, addled movements of blue grouse, feet that worked the ground like hooves, or else massaged it erotically with moccasins. One of the nights, when almost everyone had gone, I thought I heard women singing. It turned out to be teenage boys whose strange, hoarse voices convulsed and ululated in a falsetto. Gary was there and he drummed and danced and his son and wife danced, all the repetitions redoubled by multiple generations. How affectionately the shimmering beadwork traced the shapes of their dreams and threaded them back to the bodies that dreamed them.

It had been raining on and off all evening. The spectators and all but a few dancers had left. Shoals of garbage—pop cans, hot-dog wrappers, corn husks, and pieces of fry bread— drifted up against the wooden benches. I knew I had been riding an ebb tide here at Crow Fair. I'd seen bead workers' beadwork, dancers' dance steps, Indianness for the sake of being Indian—a shell of a culture whose spontaneous force had been revived against great odds and was transmitting weak signals. But transmitting nonetheless. The last inter-tribal dance was announced. Already, three of the drum groups had packed up and were leaving the arbor when five or six Crow men, dressed like cowboys, walked onto the grass. In boots, not moccasins, and still smoking cigarettes, they formed a long line and shuffled around and around. The shrill, trembling song that accompanied them could empower anyone listening to turn away from distraction and slide their hands across the buttocks of the world—above and beyond the ceremonial decor that was, after all, the point of all this. At the last minute, a young boy jumped up and burst into a boiling, hot-stepping Fast Dance, his feathered headdress shaking down his back like lightning. I wondered how much of this culture-straddling he could take and what in it would finally be instructive to him. Almost under his bounding feet a row of young children were sleeping on blankets laid out for them. Their feather bustles were bent and askew and a couple of moccasins were missing. A very tall Crow man with long braids but skin so light he might actually have been white began picking up the children. One by one, and so gently none of them woke, he carried them away.

A STORM,
THE CORNFIELD,
AND ELK

Last week a bank of clouds lowered itself down summer's green ladder and let loose with a storm. A heavy snow can act like fists: trees are pummeled, hay- and grainfields are flattened, splayed out like deer beds; field corn, jackknifed and bleached blond by the freeze, is bedraggled by the brawl. All night we heard groans and crashes of cottonwood trunks snapping. "I slept under the damned kitchen table," one rancher told me. "I've already had one of them trees come through my roof." Along the highway electric lines were looped to the ground like dropped reins.

As the storm blows east toward the Dakotas, the blue of the sky intensifies. It inks dry washes and broad grasslands with quiet. In their most complete gesture of restraint, cottonwoods, willows, and wild rose engorge themselves with every hue of ruddiness—russet, puce, umber, gold, musteline—whose spectral repletion we know also to be an agony, riding oncoming waves of cold.

The French call the autumn leaf *feuille morte*. When the leaves are finally corrupted by frost they rain down into themselves until the tree, disowning itself, goes bald.

All through autumn we hear a double voice: one says everything is ripe; the other says everything is dying. The paradox is exquisite. We feel what the Japanese call "aware"—an almost untranslatable word meaning something like "beauty tinged with sadness." Some days we have to shoulder against a marauding melancholy. Dreams have a hallucinatory effect: in one, a man who is dying watches from inside a huge cocoon while stud colts run through deep mud, their balls bursting open, their seed spilling onto the black ground. My reading brings me this thought from the mad Zen priest Ikkyu: "Remember that under the skin you fondle lie the bones, waiting to reveal themselves." But another day, I ride in the mountains. Against rimrock, tall aspens have the graceful bearing of giraffes, and another small grove, not yet turned, gives off a virginal limelight that transpierces everything heavy.

Fall is the end of a rancher's year. Third and fourth cuttings of hay are stacked; cattle and sheep are gathered, weaned, and shipped; yearling bulls and horse colts are sold. "We always like this time of year, but it's a lot more fun when the cattle prices are up!" a third-generation rancher tells me.

This week I help round up their cows and calves on the Big Horns. The storm system that brought three feet of snow at the beginning of the month now brings intense and continual rain. Riding for cows resembles a wild game of touch football played on skis: cows and cowboys bang into each other, or else, as the calves run back, the horse just slides. Twice today my buckskin falls with me, crushing my leg against a steep sidehill, but the mud and snow, now trampled into a gruel, is so deep it's almost impossible to get bruised.

When the cattle are finally gathered, we wean the calves from the cows in portable corrals by the road. Here, black mud reaches our shins. The stock dogs have to swim in order to move. Once, while trying to dodge a cow, my feet stuck, and losing both boots in the effort to get out of the way, I had to climb the fence barefooted. Weaning is noisy; cows don't hide their grief. As calves are loaded into semis and stock trucks, their mothers—five or six hundred of them at a time—crowd around the sorting alleys with outstretched necks, their squared-off faces all opened in a collective bellowing.

On the way home a neighboring rancher who trails his steers down the mountain highway loses one as they ride through town. There's a high-speed chase across lawns and flower beds, around the general store and the fire station. Going at a full lope, the steer ducks behind the fire truck just as Mike tries to rope him. "Missing something?" a friend yells out her window as the second loop sails like a burning hoop to the ground.

"That's nothing," one onlooker remarks. "When we brought our cattle through Kaycee one year, the minister opened the church door to see what all the noise was about and one old cow just ran in past him. He had a hell of a time getting her out."

In the valley, harvest is on but it's soggy. The pinto bean crops are sprouting, and the sugar beets are balled up with mud so that one is indistinguishable from the other. Now I can only think of mud as being sweet. At night the moon makes a brief appearance between storms and laces mud with a confectionary light. Farmers whose last cutting of hay is still on the ground turn windrows to dry as if they were limp, bedridden bodies. The hay that has already been baled is damp, and after four inches of rain (in a county where there's never more than eight inches a year) mold eats its way to the top again.

The morning sky looks like cheese. Its cobalt wheel has been cut down and all the richness of the season is at our feet. The quick-blanch of frost stings autumn's rouge into a skin that is tawny. At dawn, mowed hay meadows are the color of pumpkins, and the willows, leafless now, are pink and silver batons conducting inaudible river music. When I dress for the day, my body, white and suddenly numb, looks like dead coral.

After breakfast there are autumn chores to finish. We grease head gates on irrigation ditches, roll up tarp dams, pull horseshoes, and truck horses to their winter pasture. The harvest moon gives way to the hunter's moon. Elk, deer, and moose hunters repopulate the mountains now that the livestock is gone. One young hunting guide has already been hurt. While he was alone at camp, his horse kicked him in the spleen. Immobilized, he scratched an SOS with the sharp point of a bullet on a piece of leather he cut from his chaps. "Hurt bad. In pain. Bring doctor with painkiller," it read. Then he tied the note to the horse's halter and threw rocks at the horse until it trotted out of camp. When the horse wandered into a ranch yard down the mountain, the note was quickly discovered and a doctor was helicoptered to camp. Amid orgiastic gunfire, sometimes lives are saved.

October lifts over our heads whatever river noise is left. Long carrier waves of clouds seem to emanate from hidden reefs.

There's a logjam of them around the mountains, and the horizon appears to drop seven thousand feet. Though the rain has stopped, the road ruts are filled to the brim. I saw a frog jump cheerfully into one of them. Once in a while the mist clears and we can see the dark edge of a canyon or an island of vertical rimrock in the white bulk of snow. Up there, bull elk have been fighting all fall over harems. They charge with antlered heads, scraping the last of the life-giving velvet off, until one bull wins and trots into the private timber to mount his prize, standing almost humanly erect on hind legs while holding a cow elk's hips with his hooves.

In the fall, my life, too, is timbered, an unaccountably libidinous place: damp, overripe, and fading. The sky's congestion allows the eye's iris to open wider. The cornfield in front of me is torn parchment paper, as brittle as bougainvillea leaves whose tropical color has somehow climbed these northern stalks. I zigzag through the rows as if they were city streets. Now I want to lie down in the muddy furrows, under the frictional sawing of stalks, under corncobs which look like erections, and out of whose loose husks sprays of bronze silk dangle down.

Autumn teaches us that fruition is also death; that ripeness is a form of decay. The willows, having stood for so long near water, begin to rust. Leaves are verbs that conjugate the seasons.

Today the sky is a wafer. Placed on my tongue, it is a wholeness that has already disintegrated; placed under the tongue, it makes my heart beat strongly enough to stretch myself over the winter brilliances to come. Now I feel the tenderness to which this season rots. Its defenselessness can no longer be corrupted. Death is its purity, its sweet mud. The string of storms that came across Wyoming like elephants tied tail to trunk falters now and bleeds into a stillness.

There is neither sun, nor wind, nor snow falling. The hunters are gone; snow geese waddle in grainfields. Already, the elk have started moving out of the mountains toward sheltered feed-grounds. Their great antlers will soon fall off like chandeliers shaken from ballroom ceilings. With them the light of these autumn days, bathed in what Tennyson called "a mockery of sunshine," will go completely out.

FOR THE BEST IN PAPERBACKS, LOOK FOR THE

In every corner of the world, on every subject under the sun, Penguin represents quality and variety—the very best in publishing today.

For complete information about books available from Penguin—including Pelicans, Puffins, Peregrines, and Penguin Classics—and how to order them, write to us at the appropriate address below. Please note that for copyright reasons the selection of books varies from country to country.

In the United Kingdom: For a complete list of books available from Penguin in the U.K., please write to *Dept E.P., Penguin Books Ltd, Harmondsworth, Middlesex, UB7 0DA.*

In the United States: For a complete list of books available from Penguin in the U.S., please write to *Dept BA, Penguin,* Box 120, Bergenfield, New Jersey 07621-0120.

In Canada: For a complete list of books available from Penguin in Canada, please write to *Penguin Books Ltd, 2801 John Street, Markham, Ontario L3R 1B4.*

In Australia: For a complete list of books available from Penguin in Australia, please write to the *Marketing Department, Penguin Books Ltd, P.O. Box 257, Ringwood, Victoria 3134.*

In New Zealand: For a complete list of books available from Penguin in New Zealand, please write to the *Marketing Department, Penguin Books (NZ) Ltd, Private Bag, Takapuna, Auckland 9.*

In India: For a complete list of books available from Penguin, please write to *Penguin Overseas Ltd, 706 Eros Apartments, 56 Nehru Place, New Delhi, 110019.*

In Holland: For a complete list of books available from Penguin in Holland, please write to *Penguin Books Nederland B.V., Postbus 195, NL-1380AD Weesp, Netherlands.*

In Germany: For a complete list of books available from Penguin, please write to *Penguin Books Ltd, Friedrichstrasse 10-12, D-6000 Frankfurt Main 1, Federal Republic of Germany.*

In Spain: For a complete list of books available from Penguin in Spain, please write to *Longman, Penguin España, Calle San Nicolas 15, E-28013 Madrid, Spain.*

In Japan: For a complete list of books available from Penguin in Japan, please write to *Longman Penguin Japan Co Ltd, Yamaguchi Building, 2-12-9 Kanda Jimbocho, Chiyoda-Ku, Tokyo 101, Japan.*